Edith Sylla

Abstraction, Relation, and Induction

Abstraction, Relation, and Induction

Three Essays in the History of Thought

Julius R. Weinberg

The University of Wisconsin Press, Madison & Milwaukee, 1965

Published by the University of Wisconsin Press
Madison and Milwaukee
P. O. Box 1379, Madison, Wisconsin 53701

Copyright © 1965 by the Regents of the University of Wisconsin

Printed in the United States of America
by American Book–Stratford Press, Inc., New York, N.Y.

Library of Congress Catalog Card No. 65–16368

Georgii Sabine memoriae

et

amicitiae Radulphi Church

praeceptorum

parva pro magnis referens

Acknowledgments

I am deeply grateful to the American Council of Learned Societies and to the National Science Foundation for their support of my studies. To my colleagues in the Department of Philosophy and in the Institute for Research in the Humanities I am indebted for their encouragement and aid. I should like to express my appreciation particularly to Professors Herbert Howe and Friedrich Solmsen; to my brother, Roy Weinberg, for advising me on various points of style; to Gunther Sieburth for translating a portion of Simplicius' *Commentary on the Categories of Aristotle;* and to Dr. Claudia Kren for helping to read proof and make the index. In addition, I wish to acknowledge the great help I have received from reading the works of Simon van den Bergh, A. Krempel, and Gottfried Martin, especially in the second of the three studies presented here. To all these my grateful thanks. The extent to which I am indebted to my editor, Mrs. Joan Fleming, is beyond expression. I can only say that she is a living exemplar of patience and courtesy.

J. R. W.

Madison, Wisconsin
March, 1965

Contents

THE NOMINALISM OF BERKELEY AND HUME   3

    1 The Logical Character of Berkeley's Critique   5
    2 Berkeley's Nominalism   24
    3 Hume's Nominalism   32
    4 The Premisses of Nominalism   41
    5 Conclusions   57

THE CONCEPT OF RELATION: SOME OBSERVATIONS ON ITS HISTORY   61

    1 Introduction   61
    2 Melissus of Samos   64
    3 Plato   66
    4 Aristotle   68
    5 The Stoics   79
    6 The Epicureans   81
    7 The Neoplatonists   82
    8 Medieval Views   86
    9 Modern Views   112

HISTORICAL REMARKS ON SOME MEDIEVAL VIEWS OF INDUCTION   121

    1 Ancient Views   122
    2 Medieval Doctrines   133
    3 Conclusions   150

INDEX   154

Preface

I have attempted in these essays to throw light on some doctrines of modern philosophy by tracing certain of the ideas to their medieval sources. Some aspects of any venture of this kind are bound to be conjectural, and my case could be weakened or strengthened by examination of intermediate links. I have had little access to many of these intermediate links, and, therefore, am content to leave further work to others or to another time.

In the essay on the nominalism of Berkeley and Hume I attempt to show, first of all, that Berkeley was not attacking a straw man and, in particular, that the doctrines of abstraction (traceable ultimately to Aristotle) maintained essentially what Berkeley found objectionable; secondly, that Berkeley's attack on abstraction was based on the inconsistencies he found in the doctrine rather than mainly on his failure to discover "abstract general ideas" by his own attempts at introspection, and, finally, that the main argument for the principle tenet of Hume's nominalism, "whatever is distinguishable is separable," can be found in the fourteenth-century arguments of William of Ockham. The terminal suggestions about what was right and what was wrong with the contentions of nominalists form no essential part of the study, but seemed important enough not to be omitted altogether.

The second essay, on the history of the concept of relations, traverses ground that is not altogether unfamiliar. I have assumed that there is a correct view about relational concepts which was achieved in the late nineteenth century in the work of Peirce, Schroeder, Frege, and above all, Russell, and I have attempted to examine earlier views on the subject which I think are demonstrably mistaken and to ascertain some of the reasons and causes of the mistakes.

Whether a philosopher has tenable views about relations determines to a great extent the soundness of his views on other philosophical topics, and so the matter is of considerable importance. The doctrine that the world can be explained in terms of substances and their causal characteristics is, I think, inconsistent with the view of relations which Russell set forth clearly for the first time. But I have only attempted here to establish the historical background necessary to understand the significance and value of Russell's discoveries. If my historical account is even approximately correct, the essential correctness of Russell's work on the problem of relations would appear to be sustained.

In the third essay, I examine some of the ancient and medieval discussions of induction. The main theme of this essay is the attempt of medieval philosophers to elaborate into an intelligible doctrine the somewhat obscure and concise accounts in Aristotle. It appears that the treatment of this subject along the lines eventually developed by the Christian philosophers of the thirteenth and fourteenth centuries was started by Avicenna and was communicated to the Christian world by way of Al-Ghazali's *Logic* (which was a careful paraphrase of Avicenna's logical doctrines). It will be seen from this that the medievals anticipate the attempt of Francis Bacon to develop a logic of induction, but it will also be apparent how the medieval doctrines differ from Bacon.

Abstraction, Relation, and Induction

The Nominalism
of Berkeley and Hume

The nominalism of Berkeley and Hume and their critiques of abstraction are not only central features of British Empiricism but also pave the way for many contemporary philosophical issues. In Berkeley's case, the polemic against abstract general ideas was used to establish his thesis that *esse est percipi*, to refute the classical doctrine of common sensibles, to discredit the seventeenth-century doctrine of primary and secondary qualities, to show that such terms as *extension, matter, entity*, etc., were without meaning, and, in general, to reject views that supported materialism. Hume used his nominalistic views of language in his theories of space and time; his contention that repetition adds no new idea depends upon his nominalism; and his critiques of *cause, body*, and *personal identity* all presuppose his nominalism to some extent or other.

Hence a successful elucidation of the nominalistic views of these two important philosophers will hardly fail to be of some value.

Some explanation is called for, first for treating the views of Berkeley and Hume together, and second for doing again what has so often been done before. As far as the first point is concerned, the nominalism of Hume is a continuation of, and in some ways an improvement on, that of Berkeley. Moreover, certain features of each serve to elucidate the full meaning of the other. On the second point, the historical background of Berkeley and Hume, especially in regard to the problem of abstraction, has been insufficiently considered and also misunderstood. Thus the questions involved need re-examination.

It is sometimes forgotten that the problems about abstraction and generalization were thoroughly discussed in the Middle Ages and that these discussions had an influence which continued until the time of Berkeley and Hume despite the contempt and ridicule to which the eighteenth-century writers commonly subjected the Schoolmen. Some writers go so far as to deny this influence altogether. There have, of course, been honorable exceptions. Dugald Stewart long ago expressed some surprise that Hume himself attributed to Berkeley "an opinion, of which he was only an expositor and defender, and which, since the days of Roscelin and Abelard, has been familiarly known in all the universities of Europe." [1] And very recently, Paul Vignaux has noticed the resemblance between Hume's critique of abstraction and that of Ockham.[2] It is my contention that some aspects of the medieval discussions will throw light on the meaning of Berkeley's and Hume's views. In some instances, there is an influence to be detected which the medieval debates had on the views of these British philosophers. In other cases, reference to medieval views will bring out a tacit and latent assumption which both Berkeley and Hume make.

1. Dugald Stewart, *Elements of the Philosophy of the Human Mind* (London, 1856), p. 99.
2. Paul Vignaux, *Le Nominalisme au XIVᵉ siècle* (Montreal, 1948), p. 85.

1 · *The Logical Character of Berkeley's Critique*

George Berkeley directed his attack on illegitimate abstraction against Locke and "the Schoolmen," [3] and it is of capital importance to show that Locke and the Schoolmen actually held some of the views under attack. This is not difficult to manage. Berkeley himself quotes Aristotle as saying that "there is scarce anything so incomprehensible to me as the most universal notions because they are most remote from sense," [4] and Berkeley could have read from the same source that the mathematician "in his investigation . . . eliminates all the sensible qualities . . . and leaves only the quantitative and continuous." [5] In the *De Anima* Berkeley also might have seen Aristotle's statement that "the mind when it is thinking the objects of Mathematics, thinks as separate elements which do not exist separate" and which, as Aristotle adds elsewhere, cannot exist separate.[6] But whether or not Berkeley knew the ramifications of abstraction as Aristotle developed the doctrine, it is certain that he was familiar with it through the writings of medieval Scholastics or their followers in early modern times.[7]

3. See on this especially G. A. Johnston, *The Development of Berkeley's Philosophy* (London, 1923), pp. 118 ff.

4. *The Works of George Berkeley, Bishop of Cloyne*, ed. A. A. Luce and T. E. Jessop (London, 1948–1957), II, 130. Cf. Aristotle, *Metaphysics*, A, 2, 982^a 23–25.

5. Aristotle, *Metaphysics*, K, 2, 1061^a 29 ff. All translations from Aristotle are taken from the text in the Oxford University Press's *Works of Aristotle*, ed. J. A. Smith and W. D. Ross (Oxford and London, 1910–1952).

6. Cf. *De Anima*, iii, 8, 431^b 15 ff, and *Physics*, i, 4, 188^a 12.

7. It is sometimes supposed that Scholastic doctrines had fallen into such contempt and disrepute outside the seminaries that they were almost entirely unknown at the beginning of the eighteenth century. Thus Johnston (*The Development of Berkeley's Philosophy*, pp. 16–17): "The college in which he

It is well, therefore, to trace the main development of this doctrine through its principal representatives in medieval and early modern philosophers. Boethius, whose commentaries were textbooks in the Schools, raises the question whether, without falsification, we can conceive as if separated that which cannot in fact so exist. He adopts the solution which became the usual one and which he attributed to Alexander of Aphrodisias. We can, he holds, conceive as if separated, qualities that cannot so exist, as long as we do not assert the separation.[8]

[sc. Berkeley] lived had changed greatly since Swift's student days. Swift took his degree in 1685, after wrestling contemptuously with the 'Logics' of Burgersdicius, Keckermannus, and Smiglecius and the 'Manuals' of Baronius and Scheiblerus. But by Berkeley's time these tomes had been discarded from the curriculum, and very little attention was paid to the subtleties of the Schools. Trinity College had given a welcome to Locke's *Essay*, published in 1690, and Newton's *Principia*, published in 1687; and all interest was now concentrated on the new philosophy initiated by them." Professor Luce in his recent biography of Berkeley (A. A. Luce, *The Life of George Berkeley, Bishop of Cloyne* [London, 1949]) holds a similar view. Now I think this is both somewhat mistaken and extremely misleading. In the first place, Berkeley himself knew the works of Suarez (whom Hobbes had considered the spokesman of the Schools) and quoted from them. Berkeley's contemporary, Arthur Collier, in his *Clavis Universalis* of 1713 (Part I, chap. 1, sec. 2, VI on p. 40 of Ethel Bowman's edition [Chicago, 1909]), tells his readers to consult Suarez, Scheibler, or Baronius . . . which authors I mention more particularly, because with these I myself have been most acquainted . . . ." These "Logics" and "Manuals" were all written in the seventeenth century and, what is perhaps more important, the doctrine of abstraction under consideration was adopted not only by a majority of the Scholastics from the twelfth century onwards, but is to be found in Locke, Descartes, the Port-Royal Logic, the logic of John Wallis, and elsewhere. Since the doctrine of abstraction in Aristotle was continued without any substantial modification in Scholastic, Renaissance, and seventeenth-century philosophers, Berkeley could not have failed to know that it was the dominant view of the subject in medieval and early modern times. There is a subtlety which should not be overlooked but which does not affect the argument of this essay materially. See J. Owens, *The Doctrine of Being in the Aristotelian Metaphysics* (Toronto, 1951), p. 239.

8. See *In Isagogen Porphyrii Commenta, Editio Secunda* (ed. J. P. Migne, *Patrologia Latina* [Paris, 1844–1864], Vol. LXIV, cols. 71–86), Book I, sec. 11. R. McKeon translates this passage in his *Selections from Medieval Philosophers* (New York, 1929), I, 95–97.

This view has its ambiguities, and we can discern, as early as Abelard, two divergent tendencies. Abelard appears to follow Boethius in his explanation of abstraction when he argues that we can consider only one of the qualities which a thing has. "And when I say that I consider only this one among the qualities the nature has, the *only* refers to the attention alone, not to the mode of subsisting, otherwise the understanding would be empty. For the thing does not have only it, but it is considered only as having it." [9] This position is somewhat ambiguous, for Abelard also states that "the understanding considers separately by abstraction, but does not consider as separated . . ." [10] and this certainly sounds like the standard doctrine which we encounter in the thirteenth and later centuries. Vignaux, however, maintains that it differs, in principle, from the doctrine of Thomas Aquinas, and that it is solely a matter of fixing attention, not of conceiving apart what cannot exist apart. However this may be, John of Salisbury seems less ambiguously committed to the view that was to be the standard one. "We should not, however, fear that our understanding is empty when it perceives universals as abstracted from particular things, although the former have no actual existence apart from the latter . . . . Rather it [sc. the understanding] simply contemplates the form, without considering the matter, even though in fact the former cannot exist without the latter." [11]

Avicenna's psychological doctrine of abstraction is complicated by his theory of the illumination by means of the Agent Intellect. But on the point which interests us here, he follows Aristotle. "As to those existents which are present in matter, either because their existence is material or because they are by accident material, this faculty abstracts them both from matter and from their material

9. See "Die Logica 'Ingredientibus,'" ed. B. Geyer, in *Beiträge zur Geschichte der Philosophie des Mittelalters,* Bd. XXI, Heft 1 (1919), pp. 1–32. The translation is R. McKeon's, in *Selections from Medieval Philosophers,* I, 246.

10. "Die Logica 'Ingredientibus,'" trans. McKeon, *Selections from Medieval Philosophers,* I, 247.

11. John of Salisbury, *Metalogicon,* ii, 20, translated by D. McGarry (Berkeley and Los Angeles, 1955), pp. 119–20. See also pp. 123, 125, 137.

attachments in every respect and perceives them in pure abstraction. Thus in the case of 'man' which is predicated of many, this faculty takes the unitary nature of the many, divests it of all material quantity, quality, place, and position, and abstracts it from all these in such a way that it can be attributed to all men." [12] We find somewhat similar views of abstraction in Averroes.[13]

When we turn to the great Scholastics of the thirteenth century, the doctrine of abstraction becomes very explicit and more ambiguities are removed. Without attempting to examine representatives of all variations of the doctrine of abstraction,[14] it will be very instructive to consider in some detail the views of Thomas Aquinas. We shall discover two distinct but related principles which underlie his views. The first is this: "But what is joined in reality the intellect can at times receive separately, when one of the elements is not included in the notion of the other." [15] The other is, "Everything included in the essence of the genus must also be found in that of the species, whereas certain things belong to the latter which are not found in the former." [16]

12. F. Rahman, *Avicenna's Psychology: An English translation of Kitāb Al-Najāt Book II, Chapter VI* (Oxford University Press, London, 1952), chap. 7, p. 40. See also *Algazel's Metaphysics*, ed. J. T. Muckle (Toronto, 1933), pp. 174 and 205. Some opposition to such views can be found in Al-Ghazali's *Tahafut*, though Al-Ghazali's views are rather unsatisfactory and incoherent on this question at issue. See Averroes, *Tahafut al-Tahafut*, trans. S. van den Bergh (London, 1954), I, 64–65 and 354. It is (however incomplete Al-Ghazali's views may be) worth noticing that his theory is close to Berkeley on many points. See van den Bergh's translation, pp. 354–55. Al-Ghazali, however, as van den Bergh notices, appears to contradict himself.

13. For Averroes' views, see *Opera Omnia Aristotelis* (Venice, 1574), I, 24; II, 29ᵛ–31ᵛ.

14. For the history of abstraction among the Franciscans, see J. Rohmer, "La Théorie de l'Abstraction dans L'École Franciscaine de Alexandre de Halès a Jean Peckam," *Archives d'histoire doctrinale et littéraire au moyen âge*, III (1928), 105 ff.

15. *Summa contra Gentiles*, i, 54 [par. 3], translated by A. Pegis, *On the Truth of the Catholic Faith, Book I* (New York, 1955), p. 90.

16. *Summa contra Gentiles*, ii, 91 [par. 3], translated by J. Anderson, *On the Truth of the Catholic Faith, Book II* (New York, 1956), p. 313. Cf. *Summa contra Gentiles*, i, 25 [par. 2].

We shall encounter both these principles again in the seventeenth century. The implication of the first is plain. If one aspect of an essence is not part of the definition of another, we can conceive each separately even if the two aspects are incapable of separation in existence. The second principle is also clear: the generic is a part of the specific nature. This point can be found stated by Aristotle: "If then the genus absolutely does not exist apart from the species which it as genus includes, or if it exists but exists as matter (for the voice is genus and matter, but its differentiae make the kinds, i.e. the letters, out of it), clearly the definition is the formula which comprises the differentiae." [17] And Proclus further explains that the genus is not an aggregate of the species, but present in each of them, being prior to them and partaken of by each of them.[18]

There is one more fundamental point that must be made for an adequate understanding of Aquinas' position. Not only is it abundantly clear that, in nature, the generic cannot exist save in one or another of its specific determinations, but also that, in nature, the specific cannot exist save in this or that individual instance. "Universals . . . are not subsisting things, but rather have being only in singulars." [19] The great majority of thirteenth- and fourteenth-century Scholastics agreed that the Platonic doctrine of separate universals was mistaken. Hence the problem of abstraction was understood to be a psychological and epistemological issue. Individual things alone exist in all specificity, but the generic concept can be conceived apart from such singularity of individuals and apart from the specific forms in which alone the generic is exhibited in nature.

Many passages make clear that the generic concept can be had in

---

17. *Metaphysics*, Z, 12, 1038ᵃ 5 ff. And see H. W. B. Joseph, *An Introduction to Logic* (Oxford, 1916), especially pp. 83–84, for some remarks on the subject.

18. Proclus, *In Platonis Parmenides,* ed. V. Cousin (Paris, 1820–1827), I, 42.

19. *Summa contra Gentiles,* i, 65 [par. 2] (trans. Pegis, *Truth of the Catholic Faith, Book I*, p. 213). Cf. *Quaestiones Disputatae De Anima,* a. 1, ad 2ᵘᵐ; *Summa Theologiae,* Part I, q. 85, a. 1, ad 1ᵘᵐ, and a. 2, ad 2ᵘᵐ.

abstraction from the specific, although the former cannot exist
without the latter. "They [sc. some opponents] ignored the fact
that what is common or universal cannot exist without addition,
but is considered without addition. For *animal* cannot be without
the difference *rational* or the difference *irrational*, although it is
considered without these differences. What is more, although a
universal may be considered without addition, it is not without
the receptibility of addition; for, if no difference could be added
to *animal*, it would not be a genus. The same is true of all other
names." [20] That the operation of 'considering' one constituent of
an integral nature without the other is not a matter of fixing attention merely, is shown by the ultimate sentence of the quotation
just given, and is brought out even more clearly where Thomas
Aquinas deals especially with mathematical abstraction. When one
thing "non est de intellectu alterius . . . ideo potest unum separatim
intelligi sine alio. Et hoc est unum intellectum esse abstractum ab
alio." [21] That form is abstracted from individual sensible matter,
and, in the case of mathematical forms, from common sensible
matter, is asserted in the *Summa Theologiae*, Part I, question 85,
where Thomas deals expressly with the activity of the intellect.[22]
And it is further maintained that, in the case of *being, unity,
potency, act* and the like, abstraction is made even from the common intelligible matter of mathematical things.[23]

In fairness to Aquinas and other Scholastics it must be stated that

20. *Summa contra Gentiles*, i, 26 [par. 11] (trans. Pegis, *Truth of the
Catholic Faith, Book I*, pp. 131–32).

21. *In VIII Libros Physicorum*, ii, lectio 3, quoted by E. Winance, "Note
sur l'abstraction mathématique selon St. Thomas," *Revue Philosophique de
Louvain*, LIII (Nov., 1955), 504.

22. *Summa Theologiae*, Part I, q. 85, a. 1, ad 2um.

23. In *Summa Theologiae*, Part I, q. 15, a. 3, ad 4um, Aquinas states that
"Genus can have no idea apart from the idea of species, insofar as idea denotes an *exemplar;* for genus cannot exist except in some species" (trans. A.
Pegis, *Basic Writings of St. Thomas Aquinas*, I [New York, 1944], 166). But
this means that there are no *generic* exemplars *in God*. Human minds can
and do have generic concepts. As we shall see, this point will be seized upon
by Berkeley.

none held that intelligible species and concepts are images. And it has been recently pointed out that the cognition of the essence of material things is not achieved in any naively realistic sense that some passages read out of context (e.g., *Summa Theologiae,* Part I, q. 85) would most probably suggest.[24] In the case of material essences, Thomas repeatedly urged, our knowledge is often incomplete [25] and always somewhat indirect.[26] But when all this is amply conceded, it remains that whenever an essence is understood, it is a form existing in the soul. It is also true that Aquinas maintains that the existence of the form in the soul has certain accidents appropriate to its psychical existence in accordance with the maxim that "whatever is in something is in it according to the mode of that in which it is." [27] For, as we can read in *On Being and Essence,* "This nature [e.g., of man] has a twofold act of existing, one in individual things, the other in the mind; and according to both modes of existing, accidents accompany the nature." [28] And this, as we shall see, is of fundamental importance in what follows.

It would not be difficult to exhibit many other statements of abstraction in other medieval authors to essentially the same effect. And, for future reference, it should be noticed that Ockham and some of his followers in the fourteenth and later centuries explicitly and unqualifiedly rejected the entire doctrine of abstraction which we have been considering. But it is time now to turn attention to some writings through which this doctrine could have been communicated to Locke.

Antoine Arnauld, in the fourth set of objections to Descartes's

24. See Ralph B. Gehring, S.J., "The Knowledge of Material Essences according to St. Thomas Aquinas," *Modern Schoolman,* Vol. XXXIII, No. 3 (March, 1956), pp. 153–81, and the texts cited.

25. See, e.g., *Summa contra Gentiles,* i, 3 [par. 5].

26. *Ibid.,* iii, 69; *Sententiarum,* iii, d. 35, q. 2, a. 2, sol. 1, and *especially, ibid.,* i, d. 19, q. 5, a. 1, ad 6[um].

27. *Summa contra Gentiles,* i, 49 [par. 3] (trans. Pegis, *Truth of the Catholic Faith, Book I,* p. 180). This maxim, from the *Liber de Causis,* is frequently appealed to by Aquinas.

28. *De Ente et Essentia,* translated by A. A. Maurer, C.S.B., *On Being and Essence* (Toronto, 1949), chap. 3, p. 40.

Meditations, presents some of the salient points of the doctrine of abstraction. "But the genus can be conceived without the species, . . . Thus, I can conceive figure without conceiving any of the attributes proper to the circle." [29] And it is worth observing that in ideas there is an *objective* existence of things.[30] And in *The Art of Thinking* of Arnauld and Nicole, we also find the doctrine that "in these abstractions one always sees that the inferior degree comprehends the superior with some particular determination . . . the equilateral triangle comprehends the triangle, and the triangle the rectilineal figure; but that the superior degree, being less determined, can represent more things." [31] And it is well known that Descartes held similar views about abstraction. It is worth mentioning that Descartes notices a difference which he regards as of some importance between *distinguishing* and *abstracting:* ". . . in distinguishing a substance from its accidents, we must consider both one and the other, and this helps greatly in becoming acquainted with substance; whereas if instead one only separates by abstraction this substance from these accidents, i.e. if one considers it quite alone without thinking of them, that prevents one from knowing it well, because it is by its accidents that substance is manifested." [32] Now there is no doubt that Descartes accepted the doctrine of abstraction as applied to the simple natures of the *Regulae* and as applied to the principal attributes of created substances. It will suffice to quote one passage to this effect: ". . . there is always one principal property of substance which constitutes its nature and essence, and on which all the others depend. . . . we can conceive extension without figure or action, and thinking without imagination or sensation . . . ." [33]

29. See *The Philosophical Works of Descartes,* trans. E. S. Haldane and G. R. T. Ross (Cambridge, 1931), II, 82.

30. *Ibid.,* p. 87.

31. Antoine Arnauld and Pierre Nicole, *La Logique ou l'Art de Penser,* Part I, chap. 5. I translate from p. 61 of the 5th edition (Paris, 1683).

32. Letter to Clerselier, 12 Jan. 1646 (Haldane and Ross, trans., *Philosophical Works of Descartes,* II, 134).

33. *Principles of Philosophy,* Part I, Principle 53 (Haldane and Ross, trans., *Philosophical Works of Descartes,* I, 240).

Some of the principles of the doctrine are contained in the standard logic textbooks with which Locke would, in all likelihood, have been familiar, and the doctrine was contained in the writings of Suarez, Burgersdick, Scheibler, Baron, and others. There is, then, neither serious question of its Aristotelian and Scholastic provenance nor doubt that Locke became familiar with it in one or more of the authors alluded to above.

I have gone to the trouble to illustrate this point copiously for several reasons. Although Berkeley explicitly directed his attack against Locke and the Schoolmen, many critics have held that Berkeley's attack was vitiated by his psychologism and by a blunder which leaves the doctrine of abstraction unaffected by his criticism. In the sequel I shall admit the blunder but insist that Berkeley's argument does not essentially suffer from it, and I shall argue that Berkeley's attack is not primarily psychological in character, and so does not depend on his erroneous assumptions about psychology or about the functions of language.

Berkeley often states that he cannot find such abstract general ideas in his own awareness, and this has often been taken as a simple empirical argument. But a careful examination of all the passages will leave no doubt that this argument from introspection does not, and is not intended to, stand alone. For, as a matter of textual fact, the point that introspection reveals no such ideas is made *ad hominem* when he urges that those who defend the doctrine of abstraction do not claim special intellectual powers for themselves, so that any normal person should be capable of abstracting.

In a majority of passages Berkeley argues that abstract general ideas are impossible. As we know, Hume makes the same claim. Now Berkeley means by *impossible* or *cannot exist* what is 'contradictory,' 'absurd,' 'repugnant.' This is one of the fundamental meanings of *impossible* that we find in Western philosophy from Aristotle until modern times. It is true that there have been many confusions about *impossible, necessary,* and *possible*. But in the course of medieval thought we find, from the twelfth century onward, not only fairly clear definitions of these modal terms, but also the doctrine that the absolute power of God is limited only by the principle of contradiction. Thus God cannot violate the fundamental principle of logic.[34] Berkeley, as we shall see, accepts this traditional view, and bases his argument upon it.

However, it must be admitted that one of Berkeley's accusations of inconsistency against Locke is due to his misreading of the passage in which Locke is alleged to have held that the abstract general idea of triangle includes incompatible features. R. I. Aaron has argued very persuasively that the passage cannot fairly be read to yield the absurdity which Berkeley professed to find in it, and I think it most probable that Aaron is correct.[35] But Aaron concludes that Berkeley, as a consequence of his blunder, refuted a doctrine which Locke never held, and in this he goes too far. For, as I shall attempt to show, Berkeley's argument *explicitly* does not depend on this point,[36] and so is logically as well as textually (in many texts, at least) independent of the blunder.

In the *Introduction to the Principles of Human Knowledge*, Section 8, Berkeley says the abstract general idea of color, "retaining that only which is common to all, makes an idea of colour in abstract." Similar remarks are made about abstract motion and

34. Hugh of St. Victor, *De Sacramentis Fidei Christianiae*, i, 2, chap. 22; Petrus Hispanus, *Summulae Logicales*, ed. I. M. Bocheński (Rome, 1947), tract 1; Aquinas, *Summa Theologiae*, Part I, q. 25, a. 4 and also a. 3; Aquinas, *In Perihermeneias*, i, lectio 13; Scotus, *Opus Oxoniense*, i, d. 3, q. 4; Ockham, *Sententiarum*, ii, q. 9 *in fine*, q. 19; Ockham, *Quodlibeta Septem*, vi, qq. 1 and 6. The doctrine is also encountered in some of the seventeenth- and eighteenth-century philosophers, e.g., Robert Boyle, Samuel Clarke, etc. It is well known that Descartes is, to some extent, an exception in his conception of Omnipotence as establishing even the eternal verities themselves.

35. R. I. Aaron, *John Locke* (London, 1937), pp. 192–94; 2nd edition (Oxford, 1955), pp. 196–97.

36. In the *Defence of Free-Thinking in Mathematics*, sec. 45 (Luce and Jessop, eds., *Works of George Berkeley*, IV, 134), Berkeley explicitly differentiates between the "killing blow" of the *Philosophical Commentaries* (i.e., the point that Locke's idea of *triangle* is supposed to contain the incompatible attributes of scalene, equilateral, etc.) and Locke's statement that the idea is "somewhat imperfect that cannot exist," and bases his conclusion on the *latter* point.

abstract extension, and, in Section 9, Berkeley speaks of retaining only what is common in reference to *animal* and *body*. This Lockeian view, as is clear, is going to be rejected by Berkeley. But the point here is plainly not the presence of several inconsistent positive features of the same abstraction. Indeed the point here is quite different. For Berkeley, in Section 10, holds that one cannot "abstract one from another, or conceive separately, those qualities which it is impossible should exist so separated." [37] Nor, as we shall see, is this an isolated passage.

In Section 81 of the *Principles,* the objection is directed against *entity* or *existence* as such on the ground that it is abstracted from all spirits and all ideas. In Section 5 of the *Principles,* the objection to corporeal things is that they are (illegitimately) abstracted from perception, a point that is made again in the *First Dialogue between Hylas and Philonous.* The main objection against abstract general ideas is that if x *cannot* exist, x cannot be conceived.[38]

Such passages make it clear that Berkeley's main point is independent of his unfortunate misreading of one passage of Locke. But they begin to establish the presumption that Berkeley's main objection to abstraction is logical rather than psychological in character. Although Berkeley does argue that his introspection reveals no such abstraction as Locke and the Schoolmen affected to have found, he states explicitly that the psychological argument (i.e., the argument from introspection) by itself is not the main point. In Section 81 of the *Principles* he asserts: "That there are a great variety of spirits of different orders and capacities,[39] whose faculties, both in number and extent, are far exceeding

37. Luce and Jessop, eds., *Works of George Berkeley,* II, 30.
38. This is made clear in the Seventh Dialogue of the *Alciphron* (secs. 6, 7), in the *Defence of Free-Thinking in Mathematics* (sec. 45), and in the *First Draft of the Introduction to the Principles* (Luce and Jessop, eds., *Works of George Berkeley,* II, 125).
39. I.e., the Celestial Hierarchy. We should never forget that Berkeley was an orthodox Christian. Indeed, his main argument depends on appeal to the medieval Christian doctrine that God Himself, though omnipotent, could not produce an abstract general idea, since it involves a contradiction.

those the Author of my being has bestowed on me, I see no reason
to deny. And for me to pretend to determine by my own few,
stinted, inlets of perception, what ideas the inexhaustible power
of the Supreme Spirit may imprint upon them, were certainly the
utmost folly and presumption. Since there may be, for aught that
I know, innumerable sorts of ideas or sensations, as different from
one another, and from all that I have perceived, as colours are
from sounds.[40] But, how ready soever I may be, to acknowledge
the scantiness of my comprehension, with regard to the endless
variety of spirits and ideas, that might possibly exist, yet for any
one to pretend to a notion of entity or existence, *abstracted* from
spirit and *idea*, from perceiving and being perceived, is, I suspect,
a downright repugnancy and trifling with words." [41]

It is possible to supplement these passages with still others, and
it is important to exhibit some others in order to show the reader
exactly what the *logical* point involved amounts to. In Section 5
of the *Principles*, Berkeley states that "I will not deny I can abstract, if that may properly be called *abstraction*, which extends
only to the conceiving separately such objects, as it is possible may
really exist or be actually perceived asunder." [42] The same point
is made in the Seventh Dialogue of the *Alciphron*, and again in
Section 129 of the *Principles*, where it is urged that even Infinite
Mind finds it impossible to reconcile contradictions.

Still more indication of the character of the argument can be
discovered from the *Defence of Free-Thinking in Mathematics*.
This discussion of abstraction is important for a special reason.
For, while Berkeley persists in his probably erroneous reading of
Locke's famous discussion of the idea of triangle, he differentiates
clearly between his objection to *that* discussion, and his main objection to Locke's general view of abstraction. In Section 45 of
this essay, Berkeley writes: "To me it is plain there is no consistent

40. Cf. Locke, *Essay concerning Human Understanding*, Book II, chap. 2,
par. 3.
41. Luce and Jessop, eds., *Works of George Berkeley*, II, 75–76.
42. *Ibid.*, p. 43.

idea the likeness whereof may not really exist; whatsoever therefore is said to be somewhat which cannot exist, the idea thereof
must be inconsistent. Mr. Locke acknowledgeth it doth require
pains and skill to form his general idea of a triangle. He further
expressly saith it must be neither oblique, nor rectangular, neither
equilateral nor scalenum; but all and none of these at once. He
also saith it is an idea wherein some parts of several different and
inconsistent ideas are put together. All this looks very like a contradiction. But to put the matter past dispute, it must be noted that
he affirms it to be somewhat imperfect that cannot exist; con-
sequently the idea thereof is impossible or inconsistent." [43] And
the point is reinforced in Section 46 of the same essay, where it
is further argued that "I desire to know whether it is not possible
for anything to exist which doth not include a contradiction: And
if it is, whether we may not infer that what cannot possibly exist,
the same doth include a contradiction: I further desire to know,
whether the reader can frame a distinct idea of anything that includes a contradiction?" [44]

These passages are of decisive importance for a number of reasons. They make the main point against the classical abstraction
theories, that is, that a logical contradiction is involved. They further argue, as philosophers and theologians in Christendom had
argued (with negligible exceptions) from the twelfth to the eighteenth centuries, that even Omnipotence Itself cannot violate the
principle of contradiction. And finally, they show that Berkeley's
point does not depend on his misreading of one passage in Locke's
Essay. It was generally supposed that the absolutely impossible
is that which involves a contradiction, and that whatever involves

43. *Ibid.*, IV, 134.
44. *Ibid.* Cf. the *Third Dialogue between Hylas and Philonous* (Luce and
Jessop, eds., *Works of George Berkeley*, II, 232), and the Seventh Dialogue
of the *Alciphron*, secs. 5, 6, 7, for exact parallels. Luce has shown (Luce and
Jessop, eds., *Works of George Berkeley*, III, 291, note 1) that the omission of
these sections from the third edition of the *Alciphron* has nothing of the
importance that Fraser attached to it (*Works of George Berkeley*, ed. A. C.
Fraser [Oxford, 1901], II, 8).

a contradiction cannot be conceived.[45] How, Berkeley insists, can human beings conceive what God cannot produce? As God's knowledge is causal, anything He can produce He can conceive, and conversely.

We may well ask why Locke admitted that nothing like the abstract general idea can exist, and why Berkeley was so ready to accept the view that such abstraction can correspond to nothing actually existing. It is hard to believe that Locke meant to say that there is a contradiction in any abstract general idea. In fact, in one place Locke explicitly states that an indispensable condition for intelligibility is consistency, so that an inconsistent idea would be impossible. And here he is in agreement with Descartes, who also held internal consistency to be indispensable to distinct conception.[46] It is clear, therefore, that Locke meant only that particulars with merely generic characteristics do not and cannot exist outside consciousness. And it seems equally clear that Locke did not suppose that abstract general ideas are describable only in self-contradictory terms. And, as we have seen, the same can

45. E.g., *First Draft of the Introduction to the Principles:* "It is, I think, a receiv'd axiom that an impossibility cannot be conceiv'd. For what created intelligence will pretend to conceive, that which God cannot cause to be? Now it is on all hands agreed, that nothing abstract or general can be made really to exist, whence it should seem to follow, that it cannot have so much as an ideal existence in the understanding" (Luce and Jessop, eds., *Works of George Berkeley*, II, 125). The *Introduction to the Principles*, sec. 10, makes the same point: "But I deny that I can abstract one from another, or conceive separately, those qualities which it is impossible should exist so separated . . . ." (Luce and Jessop, eds., *Works of George Berkeley*, II, 30).

46. *Essay concerning Human Understanding*, Book III, chap. 3, par. 19, towards the end: ". . . yet supposing those names to stand for complex abstract ideas that contained no inconsistency in them, the essence of a mermaid is as intelligible as that of a man . . ." (*John Locke: An Essay concerning Human Understanding*, ed. A. C. Fraser [Oxford, 1894], II, 30). Cf. Book III, chap. 10, par. 33, where Locke states that inconsistent ideas "cannot so much as exist in the mind, much less any real being ever be denominated from them" (ed. Fraser, p. 146). Cf. Descartes, Letter to Mersenne, 30 Sept. 1640 (*Ouevres de Descartes*, ed. C. Adam and P. Tannery [Paris, 1897–1910], III, 191), and *Responsio ad Secundas Objectiones* (*Ouevres de Descartes*, VII, 152), quoted by A. Gewirth, "Clearness and Distinctness in Descartes," *Philosophy*, Vol. XVIII, No. 69 (April, 1943).

be said of the Scholastics who defended similar doctrines of abstraction. In the case of some of the Scholastics (e.g., Thomas Aquinas), explicit provision is made for this. The generic concept can exist as such in the soul but not in physical nature, since the mode of existence of any formal nature depends on the mode of the recipient of such existence. Our question, therefore, is whether, if these qualifications are taken into account, Berkeley's criticism retains any force. It can be shown, both textually and logically, that the criticism still holds.

Apropos of one example of what he regards as vicious abstraction, Berkeley asks ". . . and is it possible to separate, even in thought, any of these from perception? For my part I might as easily divide a thing from it self. . . . I will not deny I can abstract, if that may properly be called *abstraction,* which extends only to the conceiving separately such objects, as it is possible may really exist or be actually perceived asunder." [47] Hume, who followed and developed Berkeley's views on the present subject, is a good commentator here. He too argues that it is impossible to separate in conception what cannot exist in fact so separated. Such, writes Hume, "is a contradiction in terms; and even implies the flattest of all contradictions, viz. that it is possible for the same thing both to be and not to be." [48] Thus, for Berkeley (and for Hume also), there is a contradiction in supposing that the generic can be sep-

47. *Principles,* sec. 5 (Luce and Jessop, eds., *Works of George Berkeley,* II, 43). Cf. the *First Dialogue between Hylas and Philonous:* ". . . it is an universally received maxim, that *every thing which exists, is particular.* . . . Now I am content to put our dispute on this issue. If you can frame in your thoughts a distinct abstract idea of motion or extension, divested of all those sensible modes, as swift and slow, great and small, round and square, and the like, which are acknowledged to exist only in the mind, I will then yield the point you contend for" (Luce and Jessop, eds., *Works of George Berkeley,* II, 192–93).

48. *Treatise of Human Nature,* Book I, Part I, sec. 7 (Everyman's Library edition [London, 1911], I, 27). Cf. F. Suarez, *Disputationes Metaphysicae,* Disputatio VII, translated by Cyril Vollert, S.J., as *On the Various Kinds of Distinctions* (Milwaukee, 1947), pp. 41, 56, for language that is close to both Berkeley and Hume. Cf. also Thomas Aquinas, *De Ente et Essentia,* ed. L. Baur (Münster, 1926), p. 30: "non enim potest dici quod Socrates sit hoc quod ab eo separatum est . . . ."

arated, even in thought, from the specific variants of itself. For if the specific characteristic is held to *contain* the generic characteristic, and if it is further maintained that the genus can exist only in its several specific determinations, the separation of the generic from the specific is a *separation of a thing from itself* and this, indeed, is a contradiction.

That the contradiction be brought out still more clearly, let us review two points made by the defenders of abstraction. In the first place, as we have seen, the genus exists only as part of the species which, in turn, exists only as the nature of individuals. In the second place, since the definition of the genus does not include any of the specific differentiae, it can be understood without these differentiae. To understand the genus, however, is to have an abstract concept which is the proper and peculiar referent of the generic name. The actual separation of genus from species in nature, it is agreed, is a contradiction, because the species contain the genus as an inseparable part. The specific difference cannot exist save as determination of a genus, and the genus cannot be save within a species. But the doctrine of abstraction holds that the genus-concept exists in separation from the species. This is to separate some feature of reality from itself.

Thus Berkeley is saying that to separate the specific from the generic, on the assumption that the generic is a part of the specific, is to separate a thing from itself. Or to put it as Hume did, it is to say that the same thing both is and is not, a flat contradiction. Berkeley does not explain how generic ideas occur, and Hume's explanation [49] does not clearly differentiate between exact and approximate resemblance. But it does not matter at this place what their own positive theories are. The point of interest here is only whether Berkeley was correct in supposing that the defenders of abstract general ideas were guilty of a contradiction. And this, I think, he successfully established.

It is also of interest, of course, to know whether, on any descrip-

49. See *Treatise of Human Nature*, Book I, Part I, sec. 7, the long footnote (Everyman ed., I, 28) and the section as a whole (Everyman ed., I, 25–33).

tion of the relation of generic and specific concepts, it is possible to understand the generic without understanding some specific concept subsumed under it. Here we must make a distinction. A generic image does seem impossible on logical grounds. For the sort of statement which we commonly make about generic resemblance involves a *multiplicity* of resembling items, none of which is the exact duplicate of any other. A single integral item which would adequately exhibit such a multiplicity is, therefore, out of the question. For it is just as if we were to attempt to exhibit a dyadic relation by means of a one-place predicate expression.

"The genus is that which is predicated of many as the *material* or common *part* of their essence, as, e.g., *animal*. The differentia is that which is predicated of many as the *formal* or discretive *part* of the essence, as, for example, *rational*. The species is predicated as the *whole essence*, as, e.g., man." [50] The genus, therefore, cannot exist without the several species of which it is a part only. Whatever *can* exist, involves no contradiction. The existence of a concept in the mind is the existence of some particular of a formal character. The generic concept cannot be abstracted from specific concepts without contradiction.

Berkeley (Hume too, as we shall point out later) assumes as a 'universally received maxim' that whatever exists is particular. And by *particular* he plainly meant both (1) what is numerically one and (2) what is completely determinate. And it is sometimes supposed that he thus begs the whole question. We must insist that this is not true. Most of the Scholastics made the first part of the assumption, viz., that whatever exists is numerically single. But quite apart from this, it ought to be clear by this time that Berkeley's polemic against Locke and the Schoolmen does not proceed from assumptions which Berkeley himself lays down. There is, or so it seems, an inconsistency in the doctrine of abstraction as maintained by its several adherents. For if it is true

50. *Artis logicae Compendium in usum Juventutis academicae,* editio nova, correct. et emendat. (Oxford: J. Fletcher, 1793), pp. 10 ff.

that the generic cannot exist apart from the specific, that concepts are forms or 'objects' in the mind, and that what 'cannot exist' is what involves contradiction, surely Berkeley has made the point that an existent in the mind that has only a generic characteristic is a contradiction in terms.

It is true that, in some of the passages in which Locke discusses the question of abstract general ideas, he seems to hold a view of them that is immune to Berkeley's criticism. The species is, for Locke, often a complex idea composed of several mutually independent ideas. Thus species S_1 is composed of ideas $i_1, i_2, \ldots i_n$, and S_2 of $i_k \ldots i_l$. The constituents of S_1 are mutually independent, and likewise those of S_2. One or more of the constituents of S_1 could, therefore, be qualitatively identical with one or more of the constituents of S_2. If so, a generic concept including S_1 and S_2 could be formed. The genus of which S_1 and S_2 are species is formed by taking the constituents common to S_1 and S_2. Locke certainly speaks at times in this way. "These [sc. more comprehensive classes which by the masters of logic are called genera] are complex ideas designedly imperfect: and it is visible at first sight, that several of those qualities that are to be found in the things themselves are purposely left out of generical ideas. For, as the mind, to make general ideas comprehending several particulars, leaves out those of time and place, and such other, that make them incommunicable to more than one individual; so to make other yet more general ideas, that may comprehend different sorts, it leaves out those qualities that distinguish them, and puts into its new collection only such ideas as are common to several sorts." [51] If each constituent of every one of the specific complex ideas is wholly determinate and thus if in every specific idea there are logically independent and wholly determinate con-

51. *Essay concerning Human Understanding*, Book III, chap. 6, par. 32 (ed. Fraser, II, 83). The 'genus' which is under consideration here is actually only the intersection class of a class of classes, i.e., the product of a class of classes. As is obvious, this is entirely different from the generic concept with which Locke and others are usually concerned.

stituents, any one or more of such constituents could be separated from the rest, and used to constitute a 'more comprehensive class.' So far there is no difficulty, and Berkeley (as well as Hume) allowed this sort of abstraction as legitimate. As each member of the complex from which abstraction is made is, by hypothesis, logically independent of the other members and as each member is entirely specific, there can be no contradiction resulting from its separation from the others. But this by no means saves Locke. For there are very many undeniable cases in which Locke maintains that the generic concept is abstracted from its specific variants. Now there is no doubt that Locke allowed *this* sort of abstraction, and it is against this sort of abstraction alone that Berkeley's attack was directed.

The foregoing considerations show that Berkeley was criticizing a doctrine which Locke and the Schoolmen actually held, and that Berkeley's critique depended neither on the minor blunder for which Berkeley was responsible nor on the special assumptions which Berkeley made in his own thinking. For he professed to find contradiction in the doctrines of the defenders of abstraction, not merely doctrines inconsistent with his own.

It might seem possible to avoid the criticism, or, at least, to suggest that there must be something wrong with it by the following argument: Whenever it is possible to define one term without mentioning another term in the definition, the meaning of the one is independent of that of the other. Now where we have a consistently defined term, we have a concept of that which can exist. But *triangular* can be defined without mentioning lengths of lines, magnitudes of angles, etc. Therefore, *triangular* can be defined without mentioning 'equilateral,' etc. Therefore the concept of triangular can be had, without having the concept of equilaterally triangular, etc. And we have many authors defending the doctrine of abstract general ideas who adopt such an argument.[52] However,

52. For instance, this consideration is to be found in Aquinas, *Summa contra Gentiles,* i, 54, and *In VIII Libros Physicorum,* ii, lectio 3; in Arnauld and Nicole, *L'Art de Penser,* Part I, chap. 5 (p. 60 of the 5th edition).

the fact that in some sense or other it is possible to "think" in terms of *triangular* without adding further determinations, does not imply that there is an object of awareness which is merely generic and in no way specific in character.

Both Berkeley and Hume attempt to deal with objections of this sort. Now that I have removed one of the main obstacles to a correct understanding of Berkeley's polemic against abstraction, it is time to expound the nominalistic views of Berkeley and Hume systematically.

2 · *Berkeley's Nominalism*

Berkeley's attack on the classical doctrines of abstraction and his nominalistic substitute explanation of the function of general terms is systematically stated in the *Introduction to the Principles*, and briefly illuminated, as we have seen, throughout his other philosophical writings. I shall, in the main, follow the theory as given in the *Introduction*.

Berkeley finds some main difficulties in philosophy to depend on what he regards as a radically mistaken theory about language. This is the doctrine that abstract general terms refer to abstract general ideas. His proposed remedy is a different (although not a new) theory about the way in which abstract terms function. And he conceives his preliminary task to be a refutation of the theory of abstract general ideas. Accordingly, he begins by stating that he, personally, is quite unable to discover by introspection such abstract general ideas. Elsewhere, as has already been noticed, his own failure to discover abstract general ideas leads him to further investigation, inasmuch as the defenders of abstraction do not claim special intellectual powers above the generality of mankind. This further investigation is, therefore, undertaken, and it reveals, to Berkeley at least, why his introspection failed. For Berkeley finds inconsistencies in the descriptions of the allegedly abstract general ideas which would make it impossible for any such to exist. The most important of these inconsistencies has been discussed in detail and it remains only to put it in the context of Berkeley's whole argument.

There are, according to Berkeley, two different sorts of abstractions which are vicious. The first: In Section 7 of the *Introduction to the Principles,* he asks whether particular colors can be abstracted from particular extensions (or the converse). The second: In Section 8, Berkeley asks whether extension in general (or color in general, etc.) can exist apart from particular extensions (or particular colors, etc.). It is important to notice that *particular* here means both 'numerically one' and 'qualitatively wholly determinate.' It has been established above that the argument against the second sort of abstraction depends in no way on particular features of Berkeley's philosophy, but depends rather on the discovery of a contradiction in the assumptions of the abstractionists themselves. Berkeley argues against the first sort of abstraction in several places, notably in the *New Theory of Vision,*[53] but, as this does not directly concern me in this eassy, I shall only observe that the arguments do not seem to me to be conclusive. Hume, as we shall see later, goes so far as to deny that we can distinguish the hue and shape of a visual datum until the *distinction of reason* has been established by complicated comparisons and habits.

After disposing of abstractions he regarded as vicious, Berkeley attempted an explanation of the widespread belief in abstract general ideas. In the *Introduction,* in its final and printed form, Berkeley argues that "First then, 'tis thought that every name hath, or ought to have, one only precise and settled signification, which inclines men to think there are certain *abstract, determinate ideas,* which constitute the true and only immediate signification

53. Sections 121–46 (Luce and Jessop, eds., *Works of George Berkeley,* I, 219–30).

of each general name. And that it is by the mediation of these abstract ideas, that a general name comes to signify any particular thing." [54] This point is further elucidated: "But to give a farther account how words came to produce the doctrine of abstract ideas, it must be observed that it is a received opinion, that language has no other end but the communicating our ideas, and that every significant name stands for an idea. This being so, and it being withal certain, that names, which yet are not thought altogether insignificant, do not always mark out particular conceivable ideas, it is straightway concluded that they stand for abstract notions." [55] The *First Draft of the Introduction to the Principles* presents as a *reductio ad absurdum* the argument that there must be proper referents for each significant name: ". . . in the proposition we have instanc'd in [sc. 'Melampus is an animal'] it is plain the word animal is not suppos'd to stand for the idea of any one particular animal, for if it be made stand for another different from that [*sic*] is marked by the name Melampus, the proposition is false and includes a contradiction. And if it be made signify the very same individual that Melampus doth, it is a tautology. But it is presumed that every name stands for an idea. It remains therefore that the word animal stands for the general, abstract idea of animal." [56]

The argument of these passages may, perhaps, be summarized thus: (1) Every significant name must stand for some idea; (2) some names cannot, without contradiction or tautology, stand for particular ideas. Hence some names stand for abstract general ideas. Berkeley's refutation consists in rejecting both premises of this argument. He denies that every significant name stands for some idea and he also denies that a name which does not stand for a particular idea must stand for an abstract general idea. As he

54. *Introduction to Principles*, sec. 18 (Luce and Jessop, eds., *Works of George Berkeley*, II, 36).

55. *Ibid.*, sec. 19 (Luce and Jessop, eds., *Works of George Berkeley*, II, 36–37).

56. Luce and Jessop, eds., *Works of George Berkeley*, II, 137.

writes, ". . . there is no one settled idea which limits the signification of the word *triangle*. 'Tis one thing for to keep a name constantly to the same definition, and another to make it stand every
where for the same idea: the one is necessary, the other useless and
impracticable." [57] And Berkeley perhaps makes the point clearer
by a passage in the *Draft of the Introduction:* ". . . when I say the
word Socrates is a proper or particular name, and the word Man
an appellative or general name, I mean no more than this viz that
the one is peculiar and appropriated to one particular person, the
other common to a great many particular persons, each whereof
has an equall right [58] to be called by the name Man. This, I say,
is the whole truth of the matter and not that I make any incomprehensible, abstract idea whereunto I annex the name Man." [59]

In the *First Draft* and elsewhere Berkeley sometimes states that
there are words which "may be and are often used to good purpose without being suppos'd to stand for or represent any idea at
all." [60] In another place in the *Draft*, Berkeley holds that a general
term stands for "a great number of particular ideas, between
which there is some likeness, and which are said to be of the same
sort," [61] and makes this point in the *Introduction*, as follows: "an
idea, which considered in it self is particular, becomes general,
by being made to represent or stand for all other particular ideas
of the same sort." [62]

The positive theory, thus far, may seem to have been stultified
by Berkeley's use of the words "of the same sort." For is this not
to assume *kind* or *sort*, i.e., to admit the "common nature" of the
medieval realists, the very notion that Berkeley is trying to elim-

57. *Introduction to Principles*, sec. 18 (Luce and Jessop, eds., *Works of George Berkeley*, II, 36).
58. On what this "equal right" depends I shall attempt to ascertain presently.
59. Luce and Jessop, eds., *Works of George Berkeley*, II, 127.
60. *Ibid.*, pp. 135–36 from the *Draft*.
61. *Ibid.*, p. 128.
62. *Introduction to Principles*, sec. 12 (Luce and Jessop, eds., *Works of George Berkeley*, II, 32).

inate? We must, I think, admit that the phrase was unfortunate. But elsewhere, Berkeley explained himself further on this point. In the Seventh Dialogue of the *Alciphron* he asks, "But may not words become general by being made to stand indiscriminately for all particular ideas which from a mutual resemblance belong to the same kind, without the intervention of any abstract general idea?" [63] Now, if Berkeley meant to say that 'to belong to the same kind' is simply 'to stand in a mutual resemblance,' the use of *kind* or *sort* can hardly be called begging the question. But it is unfortunate that Berkeley was not more explicit. The word *sort* itself is an echo, I think, from the author Berkeley was principally criticizing. In the *Essay concerning Human Understanding* Locke had said that "each [sc. individual] of which having in it a conformity to that abstract idea, is (as we call it) of that sort." [64] Thus for Locke, 'being of the same sort' meant 'having a conformity to a given abstract idea.' Berkeley can reasonably be construed to have replied that 'being of the same sort' means 'having a mutual resemblance' without any reference to a common abstraction. A particular idea or a word serves to bring together, for attention and recall, the mutually resembling particulars.

To summarize: When a term (word or particular idea) stands precisely for a single item, it is an individual term which names or denotes exactly that item. When a term stands indifferently for one or more items which bear to each other 'a mutual resemblance' so that any one has an 'equal right' with any other to the application of that term, it is a general term.

Here it is worth mentioning some possible historical origins of Berkeley's nominalistic theory of general terms. A fairly remote possibility is that Berkeley read some account of medieval nominalism in some of the late Scholastics who were still occasionally read (e.g., Suarez), or perhaps some account of nominalism in one of the manuals of logic or metaphysics which were still quoted. Professor Frithiof Brandt has suggested a more probable hypoth-

63. Luce and Jessop, eds., *Works of George Berkeley*, III, 334.
64. *Essay concerning Human Understanding*, Book III, chap. 3, par. 6 (ed. Fraser, II, 17).

esis in his book on Hobbes' natural philosophy. He points out some very striking parallels between Hobbes' nominalism and that of Berkeley and holds that the *Draft of the Introduction* is closer to Hobbes' account than is the *Introduction* itself.[65] Some of the important points of resemblance between the two authors may be noted. Hobbes held that an abstract image is impossible, and traces the notion of the supposition of abstract ideas to the mistaking of names for ideas.[66] His explanation of *universal* names or words is somewhat closer to Hume's, insofar as he recognizes that the universal name is associated with more than one image, but otherwise his account resembles Berkeley's.[67] Hobbes also maintained that the doctrine of common natures or essences is radically mistaken and rests on the failure to distinguish between separate things and separate considerations of the same thing.[68] Here Hobbes' account introduces the doctrine of considering one aspect of things without considering others, and comes close in his language to some of the medieval defenders of abstraction.[69] But there is just enough resemblance between Hobbes and Berkeley to make Brandt's hypothesis worth further investigation.[70]

Berkeley admits that, while a particular idea must be completely

65. Frithiof Brandt, *Thomas Hobbes' Mechanical Conception of Nature* (Copenhagen and London, 1928), pp. 239, 395.

66. Thomas Hobbes, *Elements of Philosophy*, Part I, chap. 5, sec. 8 (*English Works*, ed. W. Molesworth [London, 1839–1845], I, 60); *Elementorum Philosophiae*, Part I, chap. 5, sec. 8 (*Latin Works*, ed. W. Molesworth [London, 1839–1845], I, 53–54).

67. *Elements*, Part I, chap. 2, sec. 9 (*English Works*, ed. Molesworth, I, 19–20); *Elementorum Philosophiae*, Part I, chap. 2, sec. 9 (*Latin Works*, ed. Molesworth, I, 17–18). See Brandt's excellent exegesis, *Hobbes' Mechanical Conception of Nature*, p. 232.

68. *Appendix ad Leviathan*, chap. 1 (*Latin Works*, ed. Molesworth, III, 531).

69. *Elements*, Part I, chap. 3, sec. 4 (*English Works*, ed. Molesworth, I, 33–34); *Elementorum Philosophiae*, Part I, chap. 3, sec. 4 (*Latin Works*, ed. Molesworth, I, 29–30).

70. Although there is no evidence that I know of which connects the nominalism of William of Ockham with Berkeley and Hume, it is worth mentioning that, at many points, their conclusions are very similar. And later I shall introduce some of these resemblances in order to make clear the underlying assumptions of the modern nominalists.

determinate in its specific details, it is possible to *consider* it in its
generic aspect. At any rate, he states that in demonstrating a
property of triangles "it must be acknowledged that a man may
consider a figure merely as triangular, without attending to the
particular qualities of the angles, or relations of the sides. So far
he may abstract: but this will never prove, that he can frame an
abstract general inconsistent idea of a triangle." [71] The word *consider* was not happily chosen, because both it and its Latin equiv-
alent *considerare* occur again and again in the works of the
defenders of abstraction,[72] although some nominalists had also
employed the term. Thomas Reid criticized Berkeley for this ad-
mission. "If we consider a figure merely as triangular, without attending to the particular quality of the angles or relation of the
sides, this, I think, is conceiving separately things which cannot
exist so separated . . ." [73]

Although Berkeley emphatically denied that *consideration* involved abstract general ideas, the concession undoubtedly weakened his case, for both the psychology and the logic of 'separate
consideration' are obscure. How can we fail to attend to features
of an image if those features are ostensibly present? On the other
hand, how can attention render those features recessive and others
dominant without obliterating them? And, anyhow, is not the
notion of attention shifting in such a way nothing but a danger-
ously misleading figure of speech? For a philosopher who accepts

71. *Introduction to Principles*, sec. 16 (Luce and Jessop, eds., *Works of
George Berkeley*, II, 35). As Luce and Jessop have shown, these sentences,
though they were added in the 1734 edition, are not later views, because
the same point is made in the *First Dialogue between Hylas and Philonous*
(see Luce and Jessop, eds., *Works of George Berkeley*, II, 193, n. 1).

72. Boethius, *In Isagogen Porphyrii Commenta, Editio Secunda*, Book I,
sec. 11 (trans. McKeon, *Selections from Medieval Philosophers*, I, 95–96);
John of Salisbury, *Metalogicon*, ii, 20 (trans. McGarry, pp. 118 ff); Aquinas,
Summa Theologiae, Part I, q. 85, a. 1, ad 1[um], and *Summa contra Gentiles*, i,
26 [par. 11]; Arnauld and Nicole, *L'Art de Penser*, Part I, chap. 5 (p. 60 of
the 5th edition).

73. Thomas Reid, *Essays on the Intellectual Powers*, Essay 5, chap. 6, p.
408 of W. Hamilton's edition (Edinburgh, 1872).

the doctrine that, in thinking, we are *inter alia* inspecting images, does not a shift of attention actually involve an exchange of an image in which certain features are prominent for another image in which other features are prominent? Does not this conflict with the doctrine that images are entirely specific and determinate? These are but a few of the questions which the notions of *separate consideration* and *separately attending* suggest, and Berkeley's writings do not answer them.

Other difficulties in Berkeley's nominalism arise when we turn to his view that in thinking we sometimes use names without any accompanying ideation. That names can be used significantly as part of discourse that is intended to communicate fact without naming peculiar and proper referents has already been made out. But Berkeley goes on to urge that very often no ideation need or can accompany the use of names in purely communicative discourse. Algebraic symbols which do stand for concrete quantities often are used without calling up any concrete imagery: "to proceed right it is not requisite that in every step each letter suggest to your thoughts, that particular quantity it was appointed to stand for." [74] And in some cases "even although there should be no possibility of offering or exhibiting any such idea to the mind," signs may play a role in communicative discourse. Thus "for instance, the algebraic mark, which denotes the root of a negative square, hath its use in logistic operations, although it be impossible to form an idea of any such quantity." [75] Moreover, "signs may imply or suggest the relations of things; which relations, habitudes or proportions, as they cannot be by us understood but by the help of signs, so being thereby expressed and confuted, they direct and enable us to act with regard to things." [76] There are, according to Berkeley, no ideas, properly speaking, of any *relations*, but

74. *Introduction to Principles*, sec. 19 (Luce and Jessop, eds., *Works of George Berkeley*, II, 37).

75. The Seventh Dialogue of the *Alciphron*, sec. 14 (Luce and Jessop, eds., *Works of George Berkeley*, III, 307).

76. *Ibid.* Fraser notes that this sentence was added in the third edition (Fraser, ed., *Works of George Berkeley*, II, 513).

only notions. Hence here is an instance in which signs are necessary but in which they signify not ideas but only actions of the mind.

Finally, Berkeley notices an emotive or expressive use of names. Words such as *good* or *good things* are used to express or evoke emotion, or to elicit certain actions. Here no ideation accompanies the expression or evocation of emotion, or the eliciting of action.[77]

Now there is no doubt that Berkeley has made many important and acute observations about the uses of language. But it is equally clear that his views on the uses of names in cases where there is no ideation but in which the emotive use too is regressive or absent are radically unsatisfactory. And it is not difficult to see why this is so. There was no logical theory generally accepted and used in Berkeley's time in which the distinction between logical and descriptive words is clearly made out. Locke has little to say about the matter in the *Essay*. Yet without at least this distinction and its consequences, it is impossible to solve the problems of language with which Berkeley is concerned.

3 · *Hume's Nominalism*

Hume's treatment of abstraction and general terms is an extension of, and in some ways an improvement upon, Berkeley. After acknowledging his debt to Berkeley, Hume presents a statement of the case against abstract general ideas which departs from Berkeley's argument in a few important details.

As we have seen, Berkeley in one passage (the unfortunate blunder to which I have alluded several times) supposed that Locke's abstract general idea was intended to represent, conjunc-

77. *Introduction to Principles*, sec. 20; *First Draft* (Luce and Jessop, eds., *Works of George Berkeley*, II, 137–38).

tively, all specific variants of itself. Hume completely ignores this, and supposes that the abstract general idea must either (1) represent all specific variants of itself *disjunctively*, or (2) represent none of the variants. The first alternative is dismissed at once on the ground that the unlimited number of variants implies an "infinite capacity" in the mind. The second alternative is rejected because Hume holds it to be logically impossible that there be an abstract general idea with no degrees of quality or quantity. Hume's arguments are interesting because they go far beyond Berkeley, and, as we shall see, introduce the very considerations which moved some of the fourteenth-century nominalists, especially William of Ockham.

The first argument depends explicitly on the dictum that whatever is distinguishable is separable. This dictum is the basis of Hume's distinction between complex and simple constituents of consciousness. "Simple perceptions, or impressions and ideas, are such as admit of no distinction nor separation. The complex are the contrary to these, and may be distinguished into parts. Though a particular color, taste, and smell, are qualities all united together in this apple, it is easy to perceive they are not the same, but are at least distinguishable from each other." [78] Again, ". . . there are not any two impressions which are perfectly inseparable. Not to mention, that this is an evident consequence of the division of ideas into simple and complex. Wherever the imagination perceives a difference among ideas, it can easily produce a separation." [79] And we may understand more clearly the dictum by noting that, for Hume, where there are two numerically distinct items, there are two separable items. This is borne out by his discussions of *unity* and *numerical difference*. Numerical difference is more fundamental than 'specific' difference. For "Two objects, though perfectly resembling each other, and even appearing in the same place at different times, may be numerically different." [80]

78. *Treatise of Human Nature*, Book I, Part I, sec. 1 (Everyman ed., I, 12).
79. *Ibid.*, sec. 3 (Everyman ed., I, 19).
80. *Ibid.*, Part III, sec. 1 (Everyman ed., I, 73).

It is not necessary to cite Hume's discussion of causal connection to add further evidence that numerically distinct objects are logically independent of one another. For although Hume sometimes dwells on the point that the cause and effect are distinct in such a way that the nature of the cause does not offer any suggestion a priori as to the nature of the effect, his fundamental contention is that if the cause and effect are *in any way* distinct (i.e., merely distinct in number of both numerically and in quality), the one cannot be deduced from the other. And it would appear that when anything is distinguishable from anything else, this implies that they are logically independent.

Further elucidation of the maxim that distinguishables are separable is afforded by Hume's remarks on unity and existence: ". . . existence in itself belongs only to unity, and is never applicable to number [here meaning 'plurality'], but on account of the units of which the number ['plurality'] is composed. . . . It is therefore utterly absurd to suppose any number to exist, and yet deny the existence of units . . . . But the unity, which can exist alone, and whose existence is necessary to that of all number, is . . . perfectly indivisible, and incapable of being resolved into any lesser unity." [81]

The character of Hume's maxim that the distinguishable are separable has sometimes been misunderstood as a groundless psychological dogma, which is responsible for the "psychological atomism" of the British psychologists of the nineteenth century. My contention here is that it is not of that character, but rather a proposition alleged to be logical in character and explicitly stated in logical terms. It is true, I think, that Hume nowhere gives any

---

81. *Ibid.*, Part II, sec. 2 (Everyman ed., I, 37–38). Hume's terminology, viz., "numerically different," "specifically different," "numerical identity," etc., was standard. It goes back to Aristotle, e.g., *De Sensu et Sensibili*, chap. 6, 446^b 23–25. It is frequent in the Middle Ages, e.g., Ockham, *Sententiarum*, i, d. 2, q. 4, DD: "Identitas numeralis convenit uni soli rei. Identitas autem specifica non convenit uni soli individuo, sed convenit pluribus individuis, ita quod non praedicatur de quocumque uno, sed de pluribus" (*Opera Plurima* [Lyon, 1494–1496], reprinted in facsimile [London, 1962], Vol. III).

explicit argument by which the proposition may be established. But I hope to show that it is at the basis of Hume's nominalism and that an explicit argument for it was offered by the medieval nominalist William of Ockham. But while Hume gives no explicit argument, it is plain from many passages that the test of distinguishables is freedom from contradiction in the statement that one exists and the other does not, or that one can exist spatially and/or temporally separate from the other. Now this criterion is in no way peculiar to Berkeley and Hume. Similar views can be encountered in Descartes and in many medieval philosophers. What is peculiar to Berkeley, Hume, and to fourteenth-century nominalists (Ockham and his followers) is the doctrine that if objects are not numerically distinct they are not distinguishable and if objects are numerically distinct they can exist in mutual separation, or that one can exist without the other.[82]

I have already noticed (in the first section of this essay) Hume's second argument, that whatever exists exists in an absolutely determinate way. It will be recalled that Hume here argues, and in this he follows Berkeley, that if all impressions are completely specific in quantity and quality, the same must be true of ideas. It follows, on this view, that a merely generic idea derived from sources in impressions that are utterly specific contains the contradiction which Berkeley and Hume found in it. That this contradiction has not been admitted by many critics is due, in part at least, to the fact that Hume states his case in terms appropriate only to his own inventory of human consciousness. But as we have

82. This usage is verified by F. Suarez, *Disputationes Metaphysicae,* Disputatio VII, sec. 2: "First of all I submit that whenever two objective concepts are capable of separation in nature and in the concrete individual, either in such a way that one can remain in the sphere of reality without the other, or in such a way that one is really disjoined from the other and that the real union between them is dissolved, we have a sign that the distinction between them is greater than a distinction of the reasoned reason. . . ." (trans. Vollert, pp. 40 ff). Suarez quotes Aristotle (*Topics,* vii, 1, 152[b] 34–35), Alexander, Augustine (*De Trinitate,* vi, chap. 6), Durandus, Scotus, Ockham, Hervaeus Natalis, Henry of Ghent, Giles of Rome, and some sixteenth-century Scholastics.

already observed, the difficulty can be and has been stated in the language of Locke and the Schoolmen.

Hume's third argument starts from the "generally received principle" that everything in nature is individual. Thus a triangle that is not precisely determinate in sides and angles is a logical absurdity. From this, and again following Berkeley, Hume infers that what is "absurd in *fact and reality*" must be "absurd *in idea*" as well.[83] For, nothing of which there can be a clear and distinct idea can be absurd in fact and reality. And thus, Hume concludes, ideas are as completely determinate as impressions.

Hume's positive account of general terms depends on his theory of resemblance as a philosophical and as a natural relation. As it has been made out in detail by Professor Ralph Church,[84] Hume holds that the resemblance of two items depends entirely on the individual resembling items and in no way on any *tertium quid* with which the resembling items might be connected. Thus, though *resembles* is a transitive verb and therefore a relational predicate, it represents nothing distinct from the items that are resembling. Hume makes some differentiation between the resemblance of exact qualitative similarity and the resemblance of analogous items. In the long footnote to the section on abstract ideas,[85] Hume explicitly states that the resemblance of qualitatively distinct hues is nothing that is distinguishable from those hues themselves. Any alternative to this view of resemblance as a merely philosophical relation would seem to fall into the contradiction which Hume and Berkeley found in the classical doctrine of abstraction. For of any such resemblance distinct from the items of which it would hold, there would have to be an abstract general idea that would be indeterminate, and this, as we have seen, involves the contradiction to which we devoted much attention above.[86]

83. *Treatise of Human Nature,* Book I, Part I, sec. 7 (Everyman ed., I, 27).
84. See his *Hume's Theory of the Understanding* (Ithaca, N.Y., 1935), and *An Essay on Critical Appreciation* (Ithaca, N.Y., 1938).
85. *Treatise of Human Nature,* Book I, Part I, sec. 7 (Everyman ed., I, 28).
86. It is worthwhile to notice Berkeley's remarks on this subject. See R. W. Church, *An Analysis of Resemblance* (London, 1952).

This view of resemblance is not peculiar to Berkeley and Hume, for we find exactly similar formulations in the writings of Abelard and Ockham. In the gloss on Boethius' *Commentary on Porphyry's Isagoge,* Abelard states that two men resemble one another or agree in the status of 'being man' "according as the very individuals are mutually alike."[87] And William of Ockham states that, "It should not be conceded that Socrates and Plato are alike *in* something or *in* some things, but . . . they are alike by means of their very own selves" ("non debet concedi quod Sortes et Plato in aliquo conveniunt nec in aliquibus, sed . . . conveniunt aliquibus quia seipsis").[88] Similar views can be found in other nominalists of antiquity and the Middle Ages, as well as in Hobbes.

The main contribution which Hume makes to the nominalistic account of abstraction is his explanation of 'considering' an item which is both indivisible and simple and yet capable of diverse resemblances, and this depends on his view of resemblance as a natural as well as a philosophical relation. Not only are impressions and ideas related by resemblances considered as philosophical relations, but also by the natural relations of association by resemblance. In virtue of the fact that there is association of several items which resemble one another, and in virtue of the fact that a single item is capable of association in terms of the several diverse resemblances in which it stands, Hume explains the nature of abstract terms.

There are different sorts of resemblance which give rise to different sorts of abstraction. In analogical resemblance "even different simple ideas may have a similarity or resemblance to each other; nor is it necessary, that the point or circumstance of resemblance should be distinct or separable from that in which they differ."[89] Now as there are associations by both sorts of resem-

---

87. I use my own wording; cf. McKeon, *Selections from Medieval Philosophers,* I, 238, ll. 11–12. The Latin text reads "secundum quod ipsi ad invicem conveniunt" ("Die Logica 'Ingredientibus,'" ed. Geyer, *BGPM,* Bd. XXI, Heft I, p. 20, l. 9).

88. *Sententiarum,* i, d. 2, q. 6, EE.

89. *Treatise of Human Nature,* Book I, Part I, sec. 7, the long footnote (Everyman ed., I, 28).

blance, the generic idea, which "in an imperfect manner" represents diverse variations in degrees of quantity and quality, is a
wholly determinate particular which is associated both with other
determinate particulars and with a general word. When the general word is heard or spoken, read or written, it revives a particular idea and puts the user or recipient in readiness to recall any
of the other particular resembling ideas "as we may be prompted
by a present design or necessity." In terms of this account of abstract general words, Hume thinks himself able to explain how
we may 'consider' one aspect of a thing without considering another aspect, although the thing in question may not be distinguished into several parts.

Hume explicitly proposes, then, to employ "the same principles" to explain "the distinction of reason" as he employed to
explain the nature and function of general terms. "The difficulty
of explaining this distinction," he maintains, "arises from the principle above explained, *that all ideas which are different are separable*. For it follows from thence, that if the figure be different
from the body [figured], their ideas must be separable as well
as distinguishable; if [on the other hand] they be not different,
their ideas can neither be separable nor distinguishable." [90] This
difficulty Hume proposes to remove by his doctrine of resemblance and his theory of abstraction. In the perfect simplicity of
the not further reducible items of consciousness there are "contained" many "different resemblances and relations." Thus, while
we cannot distinguish in a colored patch the color from the shape
defining its border, we can compare the patch with others exactly
or analogically resembling it. And the colored patch belongs not
to one but to several different and disparate resemblance-ranges.
The particular shape *is* one of these resemblance-ranges, the particular hue another. The different aspects of any items of consciousness are thus constituted by the "resemblances of which
they are susceptible." Hence, 'to *consider* the color without *con-*

90. *Ibid.* (Everyman ed., I, 32).

sidering the shape of a visual datum' means 'to be activated in the habitual association in respect to one of the resemblance-ranges without being activated at all or to the same degree in respect of another one of these ranges.'

It is clear that Hume's theory of the distinction of reason was prompted by a deficiency in Berkeley's account of abstraction. The objection which Reid made to Berkeley was probably brought up and discussed earlier. And this difficulty could have been resolved, on nominalistic terms, only by the doctrine that a simple item is a member of several mutually disparate resemblance-ranges. To say that a simple item is both colored and figured (or, more specifically, maroon and circular) is to say that it belongs to two disparate resemblance-ranges, and this, in turn, means that it resembles one or more items in one way and one or more other items in another way.

The doctrine that a single and radically simple thing has several diverse and mutually disparate resemblances is incompatible with the view (which Hume explicitly holds) that the resemblance relation is not distinct from the things resembling. Thus suppose three radically simple things, A, B, and C. And suppose that A resembles B and that A resembles C but that B does not resemble C. For instance, suppose that A is red and round, B is orange and square, and C is oval and white. In this case A and B are very much alike in color though very unlike in shape, A and C are very much alike in shape though very unlike in color, while B and C are very unlike in both shape and color. We are also to assume that A, B, C, are each radically simple (i.e., in each thing there is no internal distinction between shape and color aspects). The resemblances are, again, neither distinguishable nor separable from the resembling things. Since Hume evidently holds that we discover and do not constitute the resemblances by the comparisons we make, the diverse and disparate resemblances have been, so it seems, excluded altogether. For shape and color qualities are, presumably, constituted by diverse resemblance-ranges, and these, in turn, are reducible without remainder to the items which are resembling. But these items, in themselves, admit of no internal differentiation, being radically simple.

That Hume is forced to this view is clear, because his dictum that whatever is distinguishable is separable leaves no other alternative. That there is no way to make out the doctrine so as to explain the distinction of reason is also plain. Further confirmation that the nominalistic doctrine is forced to this will be given presently, when I notice that Ockham is forced to the same treatment of resemblances of simples. The root of the trouble is the view of relations which we find in both Ockham and Hume.

There are many other difficulties with this view of abstraction. Both Berkeley and Hume simply assume, without any attempt at argument, that the ultimate constituents of consciousness are simple items which, if different, can exist in separation from one another. They further assume that every constituent of consciousness has a "precise degree of quantity and quality." [91] It is plain, in the case of quantity at least, that precise quantities, as Hume himself stated, exist only in pure mathematics. Furthermore, the assignment of physical quantities is an involved affair. Relations of objects to a standard object are involved in "precise degree of quantity." Hence Berkeley and Hume are both mistaken in assuming that the notion of *precise degree* is applicable to contents of perception or imagination. Briefly, we cannot assign the same meaning to *precise degree* of quantity as applied to images (if the phrase is appropriate here in *any* sense) and to *precise degree* in mathematics or physics. Therefore, while some sense of *precise degree* of quantity or quality might possibly apply to images, another and more important sense of the same phrase cannot be applied to images at all.

These considerations do not exhaust the difficulties by any means. The whole notion of the simplicity of ultimate constituents of consciousness requires a radical criticism. But as my main purpose is historical and expository, I propose to go on to other mat-

91. *Ibid.* (Everyman ed., I, 27).

ters, and the main thing with which I shall be concerned is the argument for the proposition that the different are separable. This brings me again to medieval sources of modern nominalism.

4 · *The Premisses of Nominalism*

Toward the end of the Middle Ages, nominalistic views on the problems of language and meaning became very widespread, and we hear of the successive struggles and triumphs of the nominalists in the universities. Both the nominalists and moderate realists were agreed that, outside human consciousness, there are only individuals. This view was adopted by a majority of philosophers of the seventeenth century. Some, like Hobbes, were forthright nominalists. Descartes, Spinoza, and Leibniz all agree on the individual character of existence outside the mind. But they nevertheless distinguish between pervasive characteristics and their modes. And Descartes explicitly identifies his modal distinction with the formal distinction of the Scotists. Likewise Locke, who accepted the doctrine that only individuals exist in extra-mental reality, allows that in consciousness there is a distinction between generic and specific ideas.

Thus it was that there were no views that universals exist extra-mentally which Berkeley and Hume felt obliged to criticize.[92] They always state, in fact, that the particular or individual character of existence is almost always accepted. In the *Draft of the Introduction*, it is true, Berkeley mentions that some people believe that common natures or essences exist apart from individuals. But he quickly adds, that "this [sc. that even things themselves could be universal] with reason is exploded as nonsensical and

92. See R. I. Aaron, *The Theory of Universals* (Oxford, 1952), pp. 18–19.

absurd." [93] Hence Berkeley and Hume, as we have seen, devote all their attention to showing the absurdity of the doctrine of abstraction. But, as we have also seen, Hume makes his positive views depend on the doctrine that different and distinguishable things are always separable. And no explicit argument for this doctrine is given. Hence it is important to trace the doctrine through its earlier formulation in order to discover the logic by which it might be supported.

The criticism of *universalia ante rem* and *in re* began in antiquity and probably among some of the so-called minor Socratics (Plato treats these criticisms as well known, and it is sometimes thought that the criticism comes from Antisthenes). In Plato and Aristotle these several objections to the doctrine of Forms are repeated in a variety of terms. Here I am concerned with only one of them, viz., the paradox of one Form in many particulars. Plato presents a somewhat crude form of the difficulty.[94] Aristotle deals explicitly with the one-and-many difficulty in *Metaphysics* Zeta (especially Chapters 13 and 14): ". . . no universal attribute is a substance . . . . substance cannot consist of substances present in it in complete reality; for things that are thus in complete reality two are never in complete reality one, though if they are *potentially* two, they can be one . . . . if the 'animal' in 'the horse' and in 'man' is one and the same, as you are with yourself, (*a*) how will the one in things that exist apart be one, and how will this 'animal' escape being divided even from itself? Further, (*b*) if it is to share in 'two-footed' and 'many-footed,' an impossible conclusion follows; for contrary attributes will belong at the same time to it although it is one and a 'this.' But . . . suppose the Form to be different in each species. Then, there will be practically an infinite number of things whose *substance* is 'animal' . . . . Further, many things will be 'animal-itself.' For . . . the 'animal' in each

93. Luce and Jessop, eds., *Works of George Berkeley*, II, 136.
94. *Parmenides*, 130 E–31 E.

species will be the substance of the species; for it is after nothing else that the species is called . . . ." [95]

We find something very like Aristotle's criticism (and explicitly attributed to Aristotle) in Boethius' *Commentary on Porphyry's Isagoge:* "For anything that is common at one time to many can not be one; indeed, that which is common is of many, particularly when one and the same thing is completely in many things at one time. Howsoever many species indeed there are, there is one genus in them all, not that the individual species share, as it were, some part of it, but each of them has at one time the whole genus. It follows from this that the whole genus, placed at one time in many individuals, can not be one; nor in fact can it happen that, since it is wholly in many at one time, it be one in number in itself. But if this is so, no genus can possibly be one, from which it follows that it is absolutely nothing; for every thing that is, is because it is one." [96]

These statements of the argument against *universalia in re* are of considerable historical importance. The problem of universals came to the medieval philosophers in the West via Boethius' translation and commentary on Porphyry's *Isagoge*, or *Introduction to Aristotle's Categories*, wherein Porphyry had stated the problem. Boethius' comments, which are plainly derived from Aristotle, are refined and developed by the nominalists of the twelfth and fourteenth centuries, especially Abelard and William of Ockham. It is worthy of remark that the fundamental principle which Boethius invokes is the convertibility of being and unity: whatever is, is one thing. The same criticism of universals and the same principle are

95. *Metaphysics*, Z, 13, 1038^b 35—14, 1039^b 11. That this criticism is, essentially, the same as the paradox proposed in the preface of Plato's *Parmenides* may be ascertained by comparing both Plato's version and the one given by Aristotle here with Aristotle's *On Ideas* as reported by Alexander of Aphrodisias. See W. D. Ross, *Aristotle: Select Fragments (Works of Aristotle*, Vol. XII [Oxford, 1952]), pp. 132–33.

96. Boethius, *In Isagogen Porphyrii, Editio Secunda*, Book I, sec. 10 (trans. McKeon, *Selections from Medieval Philosophers*, I, 93).

found in Abelard's *Glosses on Boethius*. That only individuals exist (though this includes accidents as well as substance) is fundamental to Ockham's nominalism. But it is a view that Ockham regards as established by arguments refuting alternative views. For present purposes it will be enough to summarize Ockham's discussions of distinctions, especially of the formal distinction.

Duns Scotus was the principal proponent of the notion of a *formal distinction on the side of a thing*, which is to say, an objective difference between two or more distinguishable but inseparable constituents of a single individual. It was by this means that Scotus hoped to preserve the doctrine of a common nature in diverse individuals of a kind. It is always best to let the original author speak for himself on the matter in dispute. But for the sake of brevity I am obliged to quote an accurate summary from a recent study: "A formal distinction is a distinction from the nature of the thing occurring between two or more really identical formalities, of which one, before the operation of the intellect, is conceivable without the others though inseparable from them even by divine power." [97]

An assumption to which Ockham often returns is that God can do whatever does not involve a contradiction in its accomplishment. As Vignaux has pointed out,[98] Ockham's philosophy must be understood throughout as presupposing a theology of divine omnipotence limited by the principle of contradiction only. In this way Ockham succeeds in escaping from the limits of the particular state of physical science of his epoch while at the same time requiring strict logical consistency and cogency in philosophical arguments.

As against the extreme realist position as well as the position of the Scotists, Ockham argued that "if such a thing as a universal thing were assumed, it would be one in number since it is not

97. M. J. Grajewski, *The Formal Distinction of Duns Scotus: A Study in Metaphysics* ("Catholic University of America Philosophical Series," Vol. XC [Washington, D.C., 1944]), p. 93.
98. *Le Nominalisme au XIVᵉ siècle*, pp. 82–83.

multiplied in many singulars." [99] Scotus had maintained that the common nature has some unity, "less than numerical unity," that individuals are *really*, i.e., numerically, distinct from one another, and that there is a merely formal distinction between the common nature and the individual difference in any individual. But Ockham relentlessly attacks his adversary on this point. "Wherever there is any distinction or non-identity, contradictories can be verified of whatever are distinct . . . if A and B are not the same in all ways, then the following are true: 'A is the same as A in all ways' and 'B is not the same as A in all ways.' Thus 'to be the same as A in all ways' and 'not to be the same as A in all ways' are verified of A and B." [100] Now since "it is impossible for contradictories to be verified of any unless those for which they stand are distinct things," [101] we must conclude that there is but one kind of distinction between things, namely, the real or numerical distinction. For in the first place, "All contradictories have equal repugnancy one to another. There is just as much repugnancy between soul and not-soul, ass and not-ass as between God and not-God or being and not-being." [102] And secondly, if verifying contradictories of two items does not suffice to prove them numerically distinct from one another, "every means of proving distinction of things in creatures would be lost, because contradiction is the

99. *Sententiarum*, i, d. 2, q. 4, D.

100. *Ibid.*, q. 1, D. Cf. "Quaecumque sunt idem, ita se habent, quod quidquid praedicatur de uno, praedicatur et de alio" (Aquinas, *Summa Theologiae*, Part I, q. 40, a. 1, ad 3[um] [Ottawa edition, 1941, I, 251]). "Et similiter identitas totalis non concludetur nisi per convenientiam in omnibus quae possibilia sunt attribui istis" (Nicholas of Autrecourt, *Exigit Ordo Executionis*, ed. J. R. O'Donnell in *Mediaeval Studies*, I [1939], 222, ll. 17–19). Cf. also Hobbes, *Elements*, Part II, chap. 11, sec. 1: "Now, two bodies are said to *differ* from one another when something may be said of one of them, which cannot be said of the other at the same time" (*English Works*, ed. Molesworth, I, 132). These quotations show that Ockham used a widely accepted notion of identity. This notion can be traced at least as far back as Aristotle, *Topics*, vii, 1, 152[a] 33.

101. *Sententiarum*, i, d. 2, q. 1, D.

102. *Ibid.*

most powerful way of proving a [real] distinction of things." [103]
Ockham therefore concludes that "universally as far as creatures
are concerned, an affirmation and a negation of one and the same
[predicate] can never be verified save because of a real non-
identity [= real difference = numerical difference]." [104] Ockham
therefore concludes that whatever are distinguishable within allegedly one thing make it a real composite of two things which
could, by divine power and so without contradiction, exist apart
from one another. This, then, is the argument which leads to the
dictum that whatever is distinguishable is separable.

Ockham's explanation of the resemblances on which the application and applicability of general terms depend is, therefore, exclusively in terms of the individual natures of the resembling
individuals. The likeness of items which are qualitatively or sub-
stantially alike, exactly or approximately, is not different or distinct from the resembling items themselves. "It should not be
conceded that Socrates and Plato are alike *in* something or *in* some
things; but it ought to be conceded that they are alike *by means*
of some things, because they are alike by means of their very
own selves." [105] Again, "Socrates and Plato are more alike than
Socrates and an ass. . . . But it suffices that Socrates and Plato are
more alike simply by means of their very own selves [and not in
virtue of a common nature]." [106]

Ockham applies these results as follows: Simple things can
resemble either precisely or approximately, and thus can be classified together in species or genera without assuming any intrinsic

103. *Ibid.*, q. 6, E.
104. *Ibid. Real non-identity:* Ockham uses this as a variant of *real distinc-*
tion. In this he is simply following closely the varying terminology of
Scotus. See Grajewski, *The Formal Distinction of Duns Scotus*, pp. 92–93:
"Scotus himself is not too consistent in naming his distinction: he calls it
formal non-identity, formal distinction, real distinction *secundum quid*, and
the distinction *ex natura rei.*"
105. *Sententiarum,* i, d. 2, q. 6, EE. See above, p. 37.
106. *Summa Logicae*, Part I, chap. 17 ("Franciscan Institute Publications,"
Text Series No. 2, ed. Philotheus Boehner [St. Bonaventure, N.Y., 1951],
p. 53).

complexities of the formally distinct variety.[107] The respect of similarity is not distinguishable from any respect in which two specifically different but generically like things resemble one another.

With the rejection of any universal thing or common nature and the acceptance of a similarity dependent on and wholly exhausted by the resembling items themselves (on the ground that whatever exists must be one), we are prepared to deal with the so-called distinction of reason. Is it possible that there be distinction according to a "consideration of the intellect"? Here we have alternatives: Either the distinction made by reason corresponds to some detected complexity in the thing or not. If it does, it is not a mere distinction of reason; but if not, the distinction of reason corresponds to nothing in the thing itself, which is a simple undifferentiated unit.[108] Hence Ockham rejects the notion that the specific concept contains the generic concept as part.[109] "That A and B are one thing and A is not really distinguished from B, and yet the intellect divide A from B by understanding A and not understanding B, or conversely, is impossible." [110]

Ockham developed a very elaborate and subtle theory of concepts, of which only a few aspects need be noted for our purposes. The concept is a single quality of the mind which, by its similarity to the things it is to represent, and by certain habitual connections, can stand for single things outside the mind. The various ways in which this occurs depends on the context in which the concept occurs. Its generality depends on its representative function. Generic concepts may, but need not, depend on perfect similarity. And, since Ockham expressly rejects the distinction of reason, he does not accept any distinction, within the specific concept, between generic and specific differentiating components.

107. *Sententiarum*, i, d. 8, q. 1, C, J, and q. 2; see the summary in *Tractatus de Principiis Theologiae*, ed. L. Baudry (Paris, 1936), pp. 58–60.

108. *Sententiarum*, i, d. 2, q. 2, B.

109. *Ibid.*, d. 8, q. 1, C, J; *Summa Logicae*, Part I, chap. 20, l. 22 (ed. Boehner, p. 62), and chap. 22, ll. 35 ff (ed. Boehner, p. 66).

110. *Sententiarum*, i, d. 2, q. 3, H.

Especial notice should be taken here of Ockham's treatment of the distinction of reason as applied to anything that is absolutely and unqualifiedly simple. In the case of God, many of the Scholastics held that, despite His absolute simplicity, He contains the different perfections of created beings. Hence we can attribute to God the plurality of degrees of perfection which the creation exhibits.[111] But Ockham sees in this view some radically objectionable features. And he, therefore, insists that "many things can be distinguished *by reason* [i.e., the distinction of reason] only through comparison with many outside the thing itself [sc. in which the plurality is made out]." This is proved, firstly, in the following way: "That which according to itself is one most simple thing, if it be considered merely through itself, is one most simple thing, and has to be considered according to one most simple reason; hence if, in such a being, there are to be considered many things by reason, this will occur by considering it in comparison with a plurality of things outside itself." [112] Thus the plurality of divine attributes is not a plurality in the divine nature, but only a plurality of concepts which we entertain by noticing or assuming diverse resemblances between God and things other than God.[113] In fact, Ockham explicitly argues that the simplicity of a thing in no way prevents us from including it in a genus. Simple things including no intrinsic distinction are in a genus. For in order that this be possible it suffices that the simple thing be more similar to certain things and less similar to others, so that a concept common to the simple thing and those more similar to it can be formed

---

111. Thus Aquinas, *Summa contra Gentiles*, i, 54. See especially par. 5: ". . . we must observe in the divine intellect a certain distinction and plurality of understood exemplars, according as that which is in the divine intellect is the proper exemplar of diverse things. Hence, since this obtains according as God understands the proper relation of resemblance that each creature has to Him, it remains that the exemplars of things in the divine intellect are many or distinct only according as God knows that things can be made to resemble Him by many and diverse modes" (trans. Pegis, *Truth of the Catholic Faith, Book I*, pp. 189 ff).

112. *Sententiarum*, i, d. 2, q. 2, B, ll. 25 ff.

113. Cf. *ibid.*, d. 8, qq. 1 and 2.

and also that another concept be formed common to the simple thing and those less similar to it. Thus the formation of generic concepts requires only a range of individuals which are more or less similar to one another. These individuals may be radically simple (as opposed to the composite individuals of the physical world, which are composed of matter and form). Thus radically simple qualities (of individuals) which are more or less resembling can be classified into genera and species. Ockham's views about qualities are complicated by his theory (inherited from Aristotle) of the composite nature of most qualities, and I cannot go into it here.[114] But qualities as well as substances are, according to Ockham, absolute things (i.e., a quality, supernaturally at least, can exist independent of any substance, sustained only by the conserving power of God). And simple qualities can exactly or approximately resemble other qualities and so be classified in genera and species without assuming any intrinsic distinctions within each of the resembling qualities. It will be observed that this doctrine, logically speaking, is the same as that of Hume in his long footnote to the section on abstract ideas. And we have also noticed that the doctrine of the distinction of reason is the same in both authors. As a consequence, it is reasonable to expect to discover in Ockham an argument intended to establish the dictum that whatever is distinguishable is separable.

Now it is clear that Ockham has explicitly given such an argument. It will be useful to set it forth again in some greater detail. Whatever does not include a contradiction in the supposition that it is produced is possible to the divine will. Hence wherever a contradiction can be conclusively established, there not even Omnipotence can operate. Now if a universal nature were assumed, it would have to be numerically one thing.[115] And such a

114. See Matthew Menges, *The Concept of Univocity regarding the Predication of God and Creature according to William of Ockham* ("Franciscan Institute Publications," Philosophy Series No. 9, ed. Allan B. Wolter, O.F.M. [St. Bonaventure, N.Y., 1952]); Ockham, *Sententiarum*, iii, q. 6, E.

115. *Sententiarum*, i, d. 2, q. 4, D.

universal nature could not be multiplied in many singular things. It does no good to claim with the Scotists that the unity of the universal is some sort of unity "less than numerical unity." For, as we have seen, "wherever there is any distinction or non-identity, contradictories can be verified of whatever are distinct . . . if A and B are not the same in all ways, then the following are true: 'A is the same as A in all ways' and 'B is not the same as A in all ways.' Thus 'to be the same as A in all ways' and 'not to be the same as A in all ways' are verified of A and B." Now, "it is impossible for contradictories to be verified of any unless those for which they stand are distinct things, or distinct as concept and thing. Now if the items in question exist in nature, these items are not distinct concepts, nor are they distinct as concept and thing. Hence the items are distinct things . . . now, all contradictories have equal repugnancy one to another. There is just as much repugnancy between soul and not-soul, ass and not-ass, as there is between God and not-God or being and not-being." [116] This, if sound, is lethal to realism.

If this argument is applied to the doctrines of moderate realism, especially to the doctrine of Scotus, it will follow that the common nature and the contracting difference have to be two numerically distinct things and not merely formally distinct parts of a single individual. For "if the common nature and the contracting [or individual] difference are not in all ways the same, something can be truly affirmed of the one and truly denied of the other. Now in created things the same cannot be truly affirmed and truly denied of a given single thing. Hence the common nature and the contracting difference are not one and the same thing . . ." If this argument is rejected, "all methods of proving distinctions in creatures would be destroyed, since contradiction is the strongest way

116. *Ibid.*, q. 1, D, ll. 4–27. See Paul Vignaux, "Nominalisme," in *Dictionnaire de Théologie Catholique*, Vol. XI, Part 1, both for the texts and an illuminating interpretation. Another excellent collection of texts bearing on the subject is in R. Guelluy, *Philosophie et Théologie chez Guillaume d'Ockham* (Louvain and Paris, 1947).

of proving such distinction." That the argument is intended to depend wholly on logical principles is made clear. "The syllogistic form holds equally in all matter" [117] (i.e., whatever the content of the propositions may be). It has been shown that Ockham held firmly to the absolutely formal character of logic, i.e., that the validity of argument depends only on the structure of the reasoning.[118] We have here, therefore, a purely logical argument intended to prove that every distinction is a distinction of two numerically distinct items which, however closely united in nature, could exist one without the other by virtue of the absolute power of God (which is limited only by the principle of contradiction). Thus just as in thought there is only one kind of contradiction, so in nature there is only one sort of distinction between one thing and another.[119] There can, therefore, be no universal nature which is the essence of singular things. For if such an essence were in any way distinguishable from singulars, it would, by divine power at least, be separable from the singulars and so would not constitute their essence.

Ockham carries this doctrine to its radical conclusion. Matter and form, for example, are separable *parts* of a composite substance.[120] This means that logically the particular matter of a given composite substance could exist without any form. Thus "matter is a certain thing which actually exists in the nature of things, being in potentiality to all forms although not necessarily having any . . . and therefore, matter is not to be visualized as something by itself only in potentiality which is to be actualized

---

117. *Sententiarum*, i, d. 2, q. 6, E.

118. See Philotheus Boehner, "The Medieval Crisis of Logic and the Author of the *Centiloquium* attributed to Ockham," *Franciscan Studies*, N.S. IV, No. 2 (June, 1944), 151–70.

119. Ockham, *Sententiarum*, i, d. 2, qq. 1–4.

120. Ockham, *Summulae in Libros Physicorum* (Rome, 1637), Part I, chaps. 15, 21, 23. Since some doubt has recently been cast on the authenticity of the *Summulae in Libros Physicorum*, it is just as well to note here that Ockham expresses identical views on this subject in his as yet unedited *Expositio super Physicam Aristotelis* (Berlin, cod. elect. 974). See L. Baudry, *Lexique Philosophique de Guillaume d'Ockham* (Paris, 1958), pp. 143–46.

in such and such a manner. Matter is really actual by itself and it can by no means be reduced to mere potentiality. It is always actual in the nature of things although always in potentiality with reference to the form which it lacks." [121] Moreover, "Prime matter is of the same nature in all composites, but it is not numerically one in all composites; rather in all generated things which exist at the same time there are diverse prime matters which are numerically distinct just as diverse whitenesses differ." [122] The same point holds for substantial forms and qualities. The form of one man is numerically distinct from that of another man, and the whiteness in one man is numerically distinct from the whiteness in another.

As we saw before, the majority of exponents of the classical theory of abstraction maintained that the genus is a part of the species. In accordance with his principles, Ockham rejects this notion entirely.[123] The specific concept, for Ockham, is not composed of genus and differentia. Genus and species are concepts, the former formed from singular things whose mutual resemblance is more remote than the resemblances from which a specific concept is derived. Thus there is a complete agreement between the English nominalist of the fourteenth century and the British nominalists of the eighteenth century on the principal consequences of the dictum that whatever is distinguishable is separable.

All this establishes a presumption that the logical argument for Hume's thesis has been discovered in the writings of William of Ockham. There is, as far as I know, no reason to suppose that Berkeley or Hume was acquainted with this argument or anything like it. Nominalism persisted in modern philosophy long after the explicit arguments supporting it had been forgotten.

The main argument for nominalism which is, I believe, implicit in Hume's doctrine has now been set forth. And I have suggested

121. *Summulae*, Part I, chap. 15.
122. *Ibid.*, chap. 18.
123. Ockham, *Sententiarum*, i, d. 8, q. 1, C, J; *Summa Logicae*, Part I, chap. 20, l. 22 (ed. Boehner, p. 62) and chap. 22, ll. 35 ff (ed. Boehner, p. 66).

the reason why neither Hume nor Berkeley explicitly argued for the truth of the propositions (1) that whatever exists is individual, and (2) that whatever is distinguishable is distinct and whatever is distinct is separable (and, of course, the simple converses of these propositions). It was a matter "agreed on all hands" that universal natures did not exist outside human consciousness.[124] The main task, therefore, had been accomplished, and Berkeley and Hume had only to show that the consequences, if radically carried out, would destroy the doctrine of abstraction. Hume went further than Berkeley. He insisted that the attack on abstraction was incomplete if it did not recognize that wherever there is a distinction there are two numerically distinct individuals. And these individuals are logically independent in the sense that an assertion that one of these individuals exists does not logically imply that the other individual exists. I shall try to show that the argument which Hume, I think, uses implicitly and which Ockham set forth explicitly is radically defective.

The argument not only implies that there are no qualitative universals but also that there are no relations at all. Now this shows that at least one of the premises is false, but, by itself, it does not tell us which one. And unless we can discover the answer to this, we shall be left in the uncomfortable position of knowing that one or more of certain propositions are false without knowing which they are or why. Let us, therefore, restate the traditional argument to see wherein it fails.

The common nature is not in all respects identical with the individuating difference. If x and y are not in all respects identical, then x and y are numerically different. And if x and y are numerically different, x cannot characterize y nor can y characterize x. Hence x cannot be the nature of y nor can y be the nature of x. But then there can be no common nature that differs from individuals by a merely formal difference. The eighteenth-century nominalist, Hume, put this conclusion (which he appears to ac-

124. See Aaron, *The Theory of Universals*, pp. 18–19.

cept as a premise) in similar terms: What is distinguishable is separable.

Now there are a number of aspects of this argument which are prima facie objectionable. In the first place, the definitions of the numerical identity and the numerical difference of two individuals already allow the significance of universal terms. Thus, "if there is not complete identity in every characteristic of x and y, then x is numerically different from y," when stated in more exact terminology, becomes

$$(\exists \phi) \left\{ (\phi x \cdot \sim \phi y) \supset (x \neq y) \right\}$$

and this already assumes that there is a range of significant universal terms. The use of universal terms in *this* way has been held by some recent logicians (e.g., W. V. Quine [125]) to commit the user of such a definition to the belief in universals as 'abstract entities.' This view may be open to question, but it has to be considered in any attempt to elucidate the function of universal terms. But aside from this objection, there is another, more far-reaching one. The range of 'ϕ' was implicitly restricted to non-relational predicates.[126]

If this implicit restriction is lifted, then an entirely different result is forthcoming. For if relational predicates are also involved in the definition of identity and difference, it is no longer possible to hold that numerically distinct individuals are "logically independent" of one another. This is easily seen if we consider that the total characterization of an individual x includes all its relations as well as its non-relational characteristics.

If so, the relations of a and b are involved in their each being

125. See his *From a Logical Point of View* (Cambridge, Mass., 1953).

126. My evidence for this assertion is briefly as follows: When Ockham discusses relations he notices many "inconveniences" which follow if relations are not regarded as purely conceptual in character. One of these, repeated with some frequency, is that any change of any of the relations of any one thing involves a change in all other things. Now this *is* a difficulty for anyone who maintains a substance-accident ontology but, of course, no difficulty at all for those who do not.

numerically single and numerically distinct from one another. So if relational predicates as well as non-relational predicates are allowed, it does *not* follow that whenever x and y are numerically distinct, x is "logically independent" of y. Thus, if 'aRb' is true and R is asymmetrical, $a \neq b$. But it is still impossible that $(\exists x)[x = a \cdot \sim(\exists y)xRy]$. Or, to put this more exactly, $aRb \cdot R\varepsilon asym \cdot \sim(\exists y)y \neq a \cdot aRy$ is a contradiction.

It follows from all this that the dictum that the (numerically) distinguishable are also separable is to be rejected. Ockham plainly assumed that whenever there are two numerically distinct things, say x and y, x can be separated from y without contradiction and so could be thus separated by the absolute power of God. The question is, what does "separated" mean here? It means (1) that if x and y are in some relation to one another, each can exist without continuing to be so related, and (2) that x can continue to exist after y has ceased to exist. The notion that individuals can continue existence independently of changes in their relations goes back, ultimately, to Aristotle's notion that a primary substance remains numerically one and the same despite loss or acquisition of accidents.[127] Here it is plain that a dubious analysis of relations as well as the violation of a strict definition of numerical identity is responsible for the persistence of this doctrine. For a strict definition of identity requires that a difference of any true characterization of a thing from the true characterizations of a thing implies that the things in question are numerically distinct. This eliminates individuals from persisting through alteration of qualities or changes of relation. Hence the individuals which are ultimately in question are momentary things, so that the first sense of separation (1) is eliminated. Again, if two momentary individuals are related, say R-wise (for constant R), neither can survive the exchange of R for, say, R'. This eliminates the second sense of

127. See *Categories*, chap. 5, 4ª 10 ff: "The most distinctive mark of substance appears to be that, while remaining numerically one and the same, it is capable of admitting contrary qualities. . . . The same individual person is at one time white, at another black, ..."

separation (2). It follows that the separation of distinct individuals which stand in some relation cannot be maintained. Hence it follows that the dictum "whatever are numerically distinct from one another are separable," cannot be maintained. Thus a universe consisting of temporally related elements and of elements which, at a given moment, are separably related, cannot be described in terms which justify the dictum in question.

It is now time to investigate whether the dictum that whatever are distinct are numerically distinct is true. This, I think, will also have to be rejected. There are at least two ways in which we can speak of distinction. In the first way we speak of numerically distinct individuals, and this can be established by the fact that one individual is characterized in a way in which the other individual is not. In the second way we can speak of two distinct characterizations of the same individual or of different individuals.

The notion of numerical difference applies in the second case as well as in the first. But the two ways are systematically ambiguous with respect to one another (in the sense of Russell's *types*), so that the distinctions on the level of characterizations are not significantly comparable with the numerical differences among individuals.

Now if this is so, it cannot be maintained that because there are two numerically different characterizations there must be two numerically distinct individuals. Thus from the fact that there are two distinct ways of characterizing, it does not follow that there are two individuals. Hence not every numerical distinction is a numerical distinction of individuals, and so the dictum "whatever are distinct are numerically distinct individuals" is false. Both parts of the fundamental principle of Ockham's and Hume's nominalism are mistaken.

5 · *Conclusions*

There are, I think, two main conclusions which result from a study of the critique of abstraction in medieval and eighteenth-century nominalism. The first is that there must be an entirely different account given of a process, traditionally called abstraction, which undoubtedly occurs and which is of the greatest importance in the logic and psychology of discovery. The second is that other considerations must be set forth if a nominalistic account of classes and attributes is to be maintained. And the present essay would be incomplete without at least an indication of the ways in which both these tasks may be accomplished.

Let me begin by attempting to summarize where both sides of the controversy have been right and where both sides have erred. The traditional account of abstraction, I am going to assume, has been sufficiently refuted by the joint efforts of its medieval and eighteenth-century critics. On the other hand, no one could justly maintain that even a fairly adequate account of abstract terms was given by them. The defenders of abstraction were certainly right in insisting that it is impossible to have images of 'intelligibles.' And while it is true, as Professor H. H. Price has pointed out,[128] that Hume's theory goes far beyond a simple imagist theory of abstract terms, it is not, and in principle it cannot serve as, an adequate theory of concepts. For neither Berkeley nor Hume gave any account of logical constants, and on their theories of human cognition it is impossible to see how they could have done so. In this respect, the medieval nominalists were actually in advance of their modern counterparts. In medieval logic, a clear distinction between *logical* (in medieval terminology *syncategorematic*) and

128. H. H. Price, *Thinking and Experience* (Cambridge, Mass., 1953).

descriptive (*categorematic*) expressions was quite clearly made out, and Ockham's treatment of those terms, which he regarded as admitting of merely nominal definitions, is plainly along lines which Russell later described as *logical constructions*.

It is not difficult to see why expressions defined explicitly in terms of logical constants alone or in terms of logical constants and a bare minimum of descriptive predicates cannot in the nature of the case stand for non-verbal counterparts (whether the non-verbal counterparts are assumed to be items of imagery or objects of perception). If it is agreed that the logical constants are truth-functions [129] and so serve a purpose radically different from that of indicating expressions ('logically proper names') or describing expressions, expressions definable in terms of such logical constants wholly or in part are not representative in any way that can be compared to the indications or attributions of simple descriptive expressions. Hence such expressions have no non-verbal counter-parts. Thus in the case of the expression "tree" (as used in *analysis situs*) or "hierarchy" (which is the same thing differently expressed), we have the following construction: First of all there is the ancestral relation with respect to any relation R. This is constructed thus: "x is an R-ancestor of y" is nominally defined thus: "x belongs to the field of R and y possesses every R-hereditary characteristic of x," where an R-hereditary characteristic is any characteristic f which belongs to v when uRv and when f belongs to u. Then a "tree" or "hierarchy" is any asymmetrical and one-many relation R which has a unique first term and such that the converse domain of R is the proper R-posterity of the first term of R.[130] If we list an itemized account of the terms of such a definition, we see that, without exception, all the expressions in the definitions are defined exclusively in terms of logical constants. Thus "R is asymmetrical" means "for all x, y, and if xRy then not

129. It is true that some logicians regard 'is a member of' or 'is' as a logical constant. The 'is' here in question is that of predication, not of existence.
130. See J. H. Woodger, *The Axiomatic Method in Biology* (Cambridge, 1937), p. 42.

yRx." "R is one-many" means "for all x, y, z, if xRy and zRy, then x is the same as z." "x is the beginner of R" means "there is a y such that xRy but there is no z such that zRx." "y is in the converse domain of R" means "there is an x such that xRy"; "x is a proper R-ancestor of y" is practically the same as "x is an R-ancestor of y" except that it excludes "x is an R-ancestor of x." This example is designedly a fairly complex one, although it is the logical elucidation of the relatively simple concept of "tree." This, of course, does not correspond with the psychological development of the concept of "tree," and it is true that people who are entirely innocent of the more advanced logic learn to use the term accurately in a great variety of applications. The complex adjustments which, it may be assumed, the nervous system undergoes when a concept is acquired are not yet understood in any detail, but it is reasonable to suppose that the physiological acquisitions and adjustments correspond in some way to the logical reconstruction. If all this be so, there are then two reasons why the empiricist account of abstraction is inadequate: It does not, and insofar as it is essentially an imagist theory cannot, account for the logical constants which are essential to a logical construction of, e.g., the "tree" concept. And it is psychologically inadequate because such concept-formation involves physiological events and processes which are in principle unavailable for immediate inspection and so are not explicable in terms of images.[131]

The defenders of the classical theory of abstraction were, therefore, right in maintaining that abstractions are 'intelligibles,' not sensibles, and right also in supposing some relationship between concrete imagery and the result of the abstraction process. But they were mistaken in speaking and thinking of abstractions as if they were single units of thought and so far comparable to concrete images. Locke's characterization of an idea, as any *object* of the mind when it thinks, sufficiently exhibits this tendency to

---

131. In principle unavailable for immediate inspection because the events and processes are very complex and cannot be obtained in a brief glimpse, and because we cannot get at such events and processes in any direct way.

place abstractions and concrete images on a par in some respects. But, if my previous observations are in any way close to the truth, this is a fundamental error: abstract concepts are, psychologically and logically, quite different from images, although some abstractions have a systematic relationship to concepts whose meaning is exclusively given by concrete images.

The second point of my conclusion, that different arguments for nominalism are necessary, depends on the fact that the traditional arguments of Ockham and Hume prove too much. The separability of the distinguishable principle, as Ockham sets it forth, proves that there is no extra-discursive counterpart to any relational concepts whatever. Ockham explicitly urges this when he treats of relation; Berkeley holds that we have no "ideas" but only a "notion" of relation; and Hume contends that complex ideas and impressions are exhaustively reducible to simple ideas and simple impressions.[132]

Now while it is possible to define some relational terms so as to reduce them to non-relational terms (e.g., "sm" for cardinal numbers), there are certainly undefined descriptive relational predicates which cannot be so defined. And this surely means that traditional nominalism has proved more than is warranted by the facts.

132. Ockham, *Sententiarum,* i, d. 30, and *Summa Logicae,* Part I, chap. 49; Berkeley, *Principles of Human Knowledge,* sec. 142: "It is also to be remarked, that all relations including an act of the mind, we cannot so properly be said to have an idea, but rather a notion of the relations and habitudes between things" (Luce and Jessop, eds., *Works of George Berkeley,* II, 106); Hume, *Treatise of Human Nature,* Book I, Part I, sec. 5 (*Of Relations*), point 1 (Everyman ed., I, 22).

The Concept of
Relation:
Some Observations
on Its History

1 · Introduction

It will be readily admitted that the concept of relation (which, for the moment, means that which is normally expressed in logic by an n-place predicate [n$\geqslant$2]) is fundamental to modern science, logic, and philosophy. There is no doubt, also, that the need for this concept has been felt throughout the history of civilization since the time of the Greeks. It is not, however, so readily admitted or much realized that many aspects of ancient, medieval, and early modern philosophy prevented a clear understanding of this concept. That various philosophical views were responsible for this delay in the understanding of relation is the subject of the present study. In particular I shall attempt to set forth some of the ideas and causes which account for the slow realization of the concept of relation.

The concept of relation is connected with the multiple quantification required in the correct expression of many statements of ordinary discourse as well as in the expression of propositions of mathematics and physics. There is, indeed, evidence that the need for a logic of multiple quantification was realized in antiquity. For example, it is alleged in a scholium to Aristotle's *Organon* (17ᵇ) that Theophrastus said that unless we have more than one quantification, two apparently contradictory propositions will both have to be accepted as true, e.g., "Phanias has knowledge" and "Phanias does not have knowledge." [1] Further evidence for such a need is found in some of the fourteenth-century logicians. [2] But I believe that the lack of an adequate concept of relation was one of the factors retarding the development of a logic of multiple quantification. It was certainly not the only factor, however. The need for multiple quantification would be most easily seen in connection with the notion of a mathematical function, especially as it occurs in the modern development of the calculus and its application in physics. And there is no doubt that the requirements of modern mathematical and physical science brought the concepts of relation and multiple quantification to the foreground. The retarding factors, however, must be sought in some philosophical ideas which dominated European thought from Hellenic antiquity to the nineteenth century.

There are also psychological, linguistic, and, perhaps, sociological conditions which contributed to the failure to conceive relation correctly. [3] My concern, however, is with philosophical

1. See I. M. Bocheński, *Formale Logik* (Freiburg and Munich, 1956), p. 115. As Bocheński notes in *La Logique de Théophraste* (Fribourg, Switzerland, 1947), Theophrastus did not discover the correct solution of the problem.

2. See Curtis Wilson, *William Heytesbury: Medieval Logic and the Rise of Mathematical Physics* (Madison, 1956), pp. 14–15.

3. There is, I am convinced, a *correct* way of viewing *relation*. The proof of this will be set forth later on. At present it will be sufficient to indicate the broad outlines of such a proof. (1) *Relation* as a category which cannot be treated in terms of *accident* because, as we shall see, this means that it belongs to one term or item; a relation is, minimally, two-termed, and

theories about the world and their effect on the concept of relation, rather than with causes that can, at the very best, be only conjectured.

I shall attempt to show that the various substance ontologies of the past have prevented or retarded an adequate theory of relations. In so doing, I shall begin with certain features of pre-Socratic thought (especially the Eleatics) and trace the development through Plato, Aristotle, and their successors. It will appear that Plato and Aristotle had no adequate way of dealing with relations, for reasons which lie deep in their metaphysics. Some of the Stoics denied the reality of relations in any sense, while Plotinus and Simplicius defended relations against Stoic critics. This, at first sight, looks as if some of the ancients realized the conception of relations in something approaching the modern, and, as I think, the correct sense. Yet, as it will turn out, this is an illusion. The whole argument about relation in late antiquity and the Middle Ages turns on whether there is any objective existence to relations taken as a special variety of accidents. That relations cannot really be fitted into a substance-accident ontology does not seem to have occurred to anyone.

---

no reduction of polyadic to monadic predicates is possible. The Wiener-Kuratowski method may appear to be an exception to this dictum, but, in fact, this is not the case. Hence, *relation* is a concept irreducible to any others. (2) A formal proof can be given that dyadic relations cannot, without contradiction, be reduced to monadic predicates. See C. I. Lewis, and C. H. Langford, *Symbolic Logic* (New York and London, 1932), pp. 387–88.

2 · *Melissus of Samos*

One of the main difficulties in the way of recognizing relations as distinguished features of *what is,* is derived from the Eleatic view that what is, *is one, homogeneous,* and *unchangeable.* For reasons generally familiar to students of philosophy, the Eleatics held that (1) what exists is one, from which comes the maxim of the Scholastics, *Ens et unum convertuntur;* (2) the really real (τὸ ὄντως ὄν) cannot change; (3) what is cannot come from what is not (*Ex nihilo nihil fit,* or, as Melissus of Samos put it, οὐδαμὰ ἂν γένοιτο οὐδὲν ἐκ μηδενός’).[4]

Now the various attempts of the Pluralistic systems of early Greek thought to agree with the principal contentions of the Eleatics and, at the same time, to account for change amount to two main propositions: (1) The ultimate constituents of what is do not come into being or pass away or undergo any internal mutation; but (2) change consists of the rearrangement, mixture, etc., of the many ultimate constituents. Now one of the younger Eleatics had either anticipated or observed the objection to this way out of the difficulty. For Melissus, in a fragment that has not received the attention it deserves, pointed out that "it is not possible either that its [that which is] order should be changed; for the order which it had before does not perish, nor does that which was not come into being. But, since nothing is either added to it or passes away or is altered, how can any real thing have had its order changed? For if anything became different, that would amount to a change in its order." [5] There is some slight evidence

4. Melissus, B 1, in H. Diels, *Die Fragmente der Vorsokratiker* (5th edition, ed. W. Kranz [Berlin, 1934–1937]), I, 268.
5. John Burnet, *Early Greek Philosophy* (4th ed.; London, 1930), Fragment 7, pp. 322–23.

that Melissus is criticizing Anaxagoras.[6] But whether or not this is the case, his point that any *rearrangement* involves change can be taken as a general criticism against the pluralistic system. The pluralists are thus faced with the dilemma: relations are real and undergo change or relations are not real and no change of any kind can take place. But it is clear that they maintained that all change is rearrangement or some kind of mixture or blending and implicitly neglected relation. Melissus deserves the highest credit for having seen clearly that their way out is logically indefensible.

It was possible to save change in other ways by showing the inadequacy of the Eleatic arguments or by discovering further absurdities of the Eleatic view. And these things were tried. But the subsequent history of thought is tyrannized by the idea that whatever exists is *one* and *unchangeable*.

It would be easy to show that the system of Atomism developed by Leucippus and Democritus cannot admit relations. This system explains change by rearrangements of the eternal atomic particles. Now such an explanation will work only if one arrangement is different from another and only if each arrangement is somehow a fact. But the relations of the atoms cannot be eternal elements over and above the atoms themselves, for the attachment of eternal relations to atoms would involve the familiar infinite-regress argument.[7] Nor can the relation be internal connections of the atoms, for then the atoms themselves would suffer internal change, which the system does not allow. Hence only by conniving at relations and arrangements can the system achieve any degree of plausibility.

6. Burnet, *ibid.*, p. 328, suggests this, as do G. S. Kirk and J. E. Raven, *The Presocratic Philosophers* (Cambridge, 1957), pp. 304 *et passim*. The statement that "what is" cannot suffer pain (Melissus, Fragment 7) seems to be directed against Anaxagoras' view that perception is always accompanied by pain.
7. This point was probably clear to Aristotle. See *Metaphysics*, Z, 17, 1041[b] 11 ff.

3 · *Plato*

It is clear that Plato has difficulties with relations and never succeeds in finding a satisfactory way of dealing with them. The
puzzles in the *Phaedo* [8] illustrate his first serious encounter with
the problem. There he obviously treats *Tallness* and *Shortness* as
qualities of individuals. It is true that these qualities have the odd
feature that they are qualities of *x towards* or *in comparison with*
y.[9] It might be argued that this recognition that relations are
qualities or attributes *toward* something other than the possessor
of the attributes is the beginning of a realization of the difference
between qualities and relations. But as Hackforth remarks, "this
semi-awareness of the distinction between qualities and relations is,
it seems, only momentary; from 102 D 5 onwards it disappears." [10]
It may be suggested, at least, that Plato's failure here is due to the
fact that a relation as we today would conceive it has no suitable
place in his system of thought.

The next important place where Plato discusses the matter is in
the *Parmenides* (149 E ff), and it is clear that the *Phaedo* doctrine,
if it was taken seriously when Plato wrote the *Phaedo*, is now
abandoned.[11] In *Parmenides* 149 E ff Plato subjects the *Phaedo* theory that *Tallness* and *Shortness* are Forms to a reduction to
absurdity by showing that it implies that all magnitudes are equal.
But it is not clear that Plato learned from this that the proper way

8. *Phaedo*, 102 D.
9. See F. M. Cornford, *Plato and Parmenides* (London, 1939), p. 78.
10. R. Hackforth, *Plato's Phaedo* (Cambridge, 1955), p. 155. See also F. M.
Cornford, *Plato's Theory of Knowledge* (New York and London, 1935),
pp. 282 ff.
11. The puzzles in *Republic*, vii, 523–24, seem to indicate that Plato *did*
take the problems about *Tallness* and *Shortness* in the *Phaedo* seriously.

to deal with *Greatness* and *Smallness* is by way of relations as we conceive of them. In fact, it seems that Plato's *Indefinite Dyad* has taken the place of *Greatness* and *Smallness* as Forms. But whether this conjecture is true or not would seem to depend on whether there is any independent evidence that Plato has achieved a clearer understanding of relation in other places. We may consider the discussion of *Difference* in the *Sophist*. At 255 c and d it is stated that some things are always thought of as absolute (τὰ μὲν αὐτὰ καθ' αὐτά) and some as relative (τὰ δὲ πρὸς ἄλλα). *Otherness*, we might say, is the essence of relation. *Difference* must then be distinguished as a Form in order to account for the difference of things from one another. Each of the Forms is different from the rest, not by virtue of its own nature, "but because it partakes of the character of Difference." [12] Let us look more closely into the matter. If F_1 differs from F_2 it is either (1) because F_1 and F_2 are what they are, or (2) because F_1 and F_2 partake of F_3 (i.e., *Difference*). Now assume F_1 differs from F_2.

Now F_1 and F_2 are absolute terms and therefore F_1 and F_2 differ because they partake of F_3, because whenever anything has a predicate it is because it partakes of the Form expressed by the predicate. So that F_1 and F_2 both partake of F_3 (i.e., *Difference*). This seems to be the argument. The question is: Do we have F_3 as a dyadic relation between F_1 and F_2, i.e., $D(F_1, F_2)$; or do we have F_3 as a predicate of F_1 and also as a predicate of F_2, i.e., $D(F_1)$ and $D(F_2)$? It is extremely hard to decide this, but my own conviction is that *Difference* is not thought of as a dyadic relation between two differing Forms. The language used by Plato suggests, as Cornford said,[13] that *Difference* is a Form that pervades all Forms. The *Sophist* passage cannot, then, be counted as independent evidence that Plato's treatment of relational facts was anything like the view which is common at the present time.

12. See Cornford, *Plato's Theory of Knowledge*, p. 282.
13. *Ibid.*, pp. 284–85.

4 · *Aristotle*

Aristotle is much more informative on the subject of *relation*. His views are of the greatest importance, for almost everything that has been said on the subject for the past two thousand years is, in some degree, dependent on Aristotle's doctrines.

Since he includes relation among the categories, it is well to begin with the question: what is a category? The categories are certainly not mere kinds of terms. In a number of places Aristotle seems to say that the categorical predicates indicate distinct ways in which things exist. The important point, however, is that all categories but that of substance are ways of existing which essentially depend on primary substance, i.e., whatever is in any of the categories other than substance is dependent and accidental in character.[14]

Now the category of πρός τι, of relation, is one of the categories of accidents. Aristotle says distinctly that the relative (πρός τι) is, of all the categories, the least degree of existence. It is posterior to substance, to quantity, and to quality. It is an affection (πάθος) of quantity.[15] (This does not, actually, hold of all relatives but of those involved in quantity, but I believe it entirely justified to assume that the relative is always an affection.) On the one hand, then, the relative is one of the categories of accident. Yet Aristotle repeatedly makes it plain that it has peculiar features. First of all, predications of relative terms have no meaning by themselves; i.e., it is always necessary to complete the phase so as to bring in

14. *Metaphysics*, Δ, 7, 1017ᵃ 22; Θ, 1, 1045ᵇ 32; *Nicomachean Ethics*, i, 6, 1096ᵃ 23; *De Anima*, i, 5, 410ᵃ 13.
15. *Metaphysics*, N, 1, 1088ᵃ 23.

the mention of the correlative of each relative.[16] Indeed, the essential being of everything relative is that it is relative *to* something.[17] Hence if anyone comprehends a relative he will also necessarily comprehend its correlative.[18] Moreover, it is, generally, but not universally, the case that the correlatives exist simultaneously.[19] An exception to this is in the instance of knowledge. The object of knowledge usually exists before we have knowledge, and, again, the object can exist without the knowledge of it, but not conversely.[20]

Now all things save primary substances are either present in or predicable of primary substances; if the latter did not exist, nothing else would exist.[21] Hence relation, as accident or affection (πάθος) of primary substance, exists in primary substance. Moreover, because relation is an accident, it belongs to a single primary substance or to an accident of such a substance. Nowhere is there any suggestion that a relation belongs to two substances taken together in a pair. Nor is this all. In some cases we can and must say that the relation is an accident of one term where there is no corresponding accident in the correlative. The main cases are (1) knowledge and perception, and (2) the relation of the prime mover to the object moved. In order to see Aristotle's full view of the matter we must notice two aspects of his physical theory, viz. (*a*) the nature of causal action, and (*b*) the relation of cause and effect in natural motion.

a) In the *Physics*, the case of agent and patient is distinctly included in the category of relation.[22] Moreover, both in *Physics* and in *De Anima* we are told that the realization of the agent

16. *De Sophisticis Elenchis*, chap. 31, 181ᵇ 26–28; *Topics*, vi, 1, 142ᵃ 28–31; *Categories*, chap. 6, 6ᵃ 35.
17. *Topics*, vi, 4, 142ᵃ 28–31; vi, 8, 146ᵇ 3–4.
18. *Categories*, chap. 7, 8ᵃ 35.
19. *Ibid.*, 7ᵇ 15.
20. *Ibid.*, 7ᵇ 22—8ᵃ 13.
21. *Ibid.*, chap. 5, 2ᵃ 33—2ᵇ 6.
22. *Physics*, iii, 1, 200ᵇ 28.

is in the patient.[23] Now this means that causal relation is treated as an actualization of the active potency and the passive potency in the patient, and so the relation tends to be absorbed, so to speak, into one of its terms. In so doing, Aristotle achieves a certain specious advantage. For by so doing, he has apparently established that it is *in the nature* of one thing to be causally dependent on another. Hence it can be made to appear as a matter of logical necessity that one thing depends on another and that from a knowledge of the dependent factor, we can infer that there is another thing on which it is dependent. Thus the treatment of relation as an accident in one thing somehow referring to another also explains how Aristotle can treat the definition of an attribute as containing the nature of the cause of the attribute. The familiar discussion of eclipse in the *Posterior Analytics* and the *Metaphysics* illustrates this point well.[24] The definition of eclipse, which itself is an affection of the moon, includes the cause of the deprivation of light which the moon suffers. The causal definitions of attributes are plainly cases in which *relation to something* is treated as an attribute which an object possesses.

b) Aristotle's treatment of natural motion makes the treatment of relations as accidents even more plausible. In natural motion, the thing undergoing motion has its source of motion in itself. This is a desire or inclination to move to a natural place, to reproduce, or to know. In all these cases, the relation is conceived by analogy to thought. In the case of thought, the referent is contained in the thought. And this contributes to the illusion that

23. *Ibid.*, 3, 202^b 6 ff: "It is *not* absurd that the actualization of one thing should be in another. . . . the operation is performed *on* some patient—it is not cut adrift from a subject, but is of A on B"; *De Anima*, iii, 2, 426^a 9 ff: "For as the-acting-and-being-acted-upon is to be found in the passive, not in the active factor, so also the actuality of the sensible object and that of the sensitive subject are both realized in the latter." (All translations from Aristotle, unless otherwise stated, are taken from the text in the Oxford University Press's *Works of Aristotle*, ed. J. A. Smith and W. D. Ross [Oxford and London, 1910–1952].)

24. See *Posterior Analytics*, ii, 8, 93^a 1 ff, and *Metaphysics*, H, 4, 1044^b 8–15.

there is a special sort of accident which, while remaining in one thing, refers to something else.

Only by this treatment of relation can Aristotle say the sorts of things he does about the prime mover. It moves only as being the object of desire. It undergoes no alteration, is always active, is never changed by anything beyond itself. In a word, the universe is related to God, but God has no relation to the universe. The relations of things in the universe to God are, therefore, unilateral. Such a view could be maintained only if relations are regarded as special attributes of their terms taken singly.[25]

The insistence that the basic reality is primary substance, that whatever exists depends on primary substance, that basic existence has essential unity which can only be achieved by form, and that relation is the least real of accidents since it depends on other accidents—all these propositions lead to the view of relation that was to dominate the reflections on this subject until very recent times.

The views of Aristotle on this subject are so influential that it is well to go into considerable detail. First of all, we must introduce his definitions of relation, then his classification of relations, and finally an attempt must be made to systematize his scattered remarks on the subject into something like a determinate doctrine. On certain very crucial points, in particular the point that a relation cannot be considered as a characteristic of its terms taken together, it is impossible to supply direct textual evidence. Hence it is unsafe to attribute this to Aristotle as his explicitly declared doctrine. But, as I shall argue, everything that he does say points to such a conclusion, and, indeed, it seems to be a logical consequence of his explicit views. And so it was understood by more than a working majority of his interpreters and successors.

There are two definitions of relative (πρός τι) given in the *Categories*. According to the first definition, "things are called relative, which, being either said to be *of* something else or *related to* something else, are explained by reference to that other

25. See P. H. Wicksteed, *Aristotle: The Physics* (London, 1929), Introduction, p. xxvii.

thing." [26] Aristotle, for reasons not wholly clear, modifies this by a second definition: "Indeed, if our definition of that which is relative was complete, it is very difficult, if not impossible, to prove that no substance is relative. If, however, our definition was not complete, if those things only are properly called relative in the case of which relation to an external object is a necessary condition of existence, perhaps some explanation of the dilemma can be found. The former definition does indeed apply to all relatives, but the fact that a thing is explained with reference to something else does not make it *essentially* [my italics] relative." [27]

Boethius attributes the first of these definitions to Plato and the corrected definition to Aristotle.[28] In the interpretations of the medieval Christian commentators and theologians there is much diversity of opinion concerning the import of these two definitions. They were called, respectively, *relatives* or *respects secundum dici* (according to expression), and *relatives* or *respects secundum esse* (according to existence). But some confused this distinction with another one, namely, with the difference between *relations according to reason* and *real relations*. Aquinas seems to have avoided this confusion. According to Aquinas, the difference between Aristotle's two definitions seems to be as follows: relative *terms* are, most generally considered, any terms which must be explained with reference to something other than the referent of the relative term itself. However, in a relative term *secundum dici* the principal signification of the term is not relational in character, although *secondarily* a reference to something else is made, whereas, in relatives *secundum esse*, the principal signification of the term is a reference to another thing. Thus, a term such as *knowledge* refers primarily to a *habitus* or condition of the mind

26. *Categories*, chap. 7, 6ᵃ 35–37.
27. *Ibid.*, 8ᵃ 28–35.
28. *Boethius, In Categorias Aristotelis*, ed. J. P. Migne, *Patrologia Latina* (Paris, 1844–1864), Vol. LXIV, col. 217. But, as A. Krempel remarks (*La Doctrine de la relation chez St. Thomas* [Paris, 1952], p. 396), such a formula is not to be found in the extant writings of Plato, although Plato does say things approaching it. See G. A. F. Ast, *Lexikon Platonicum* (1834–1839).

and secondarily to something knowable. By contrast, such terms as *father*, *master*, etc., principally signify a relation to something.[29] Scotus and Ockham, however, give quite different explanations, as does Albertus Magnus. Aristotle, himself, seems to have had in mind the fact that some relative terms do not require an external reference except for convenience of linguistic usage, whereas others can only be interpreted as involving the actual existence of some relation to the relative term in question.

A more important contribution of Aristotle to the subject of relation is his classification of "things called 'to something' " (πρός τι). This is given in Chapter 15 of *Metaphysics* Delta (Aristotle's 'lexicon of ambiguous terms'). The first of the three classes of relatives may be called 'arithmetical'[30] or, perhaps more accurately, relatives of comparison or resemblance. The reason why 'arithmetical' is historically more appropriate is the remark Aristotle makes here that not only *double, half, triple, third*, etc., but also *equal, like, same* all are used in respect of *one*. Thus not only is *one* "the beginning and measure of number," but it also is the basis of *equality, sameness*, and *likeness*. "Things are 'the same' whose essence is one; 'like' whose quality is one; 'equal' whose quantity is one."[31] We may question whether arithmetical relatives and the others aforementioned may be suitably classified together. But they are distinct in some ways from the relatives of the other classes.

The second class of relatives are all *causal* in nature, e.g., *father, son; heating, heated; cutting, cut;* or, generally, the active and the passive. Thus things are called relative either in virtue of an active or passive potentiality or in virtue of the actualization of such potentialities.[32]

29. Aquinas, *Summa Theologiae*, Part I, q. 13, a. 7, ad 1[um], is perhaps the clearest statement of this interpretation.
30. See G. Martin, *Wilhelm von Ockham: Untersuchungen zur Ontologie der Ordnungen* (Berlin, 1949), p. 102.
31. *Metaphysics*, Δ, 15, 1021[a] 10 ff, trans. H. Tredennick, *The Metaphysics Books I–IX* (Cambridge, Mass., 1936), p. 263.
32. *Ibid.*, 1020[b] 26 ff, and 1021[a] 14 ff.

Finally there is the class which Gottfried Martin aptly calls Intentional Relatives: e.g., *the measurable, the knowable, the sensible*. The relatives of this group have the following peculiarity: They are so-called not because they are 'to something' but rather because something else is relative to them. Thus *thinkable, sensible, knowable* all signify that something is related to them (viz., thought or sensation).[33]

No explicit place is made in this classification for spatial and temporal relations. This, it may be assumed, is because these, in Aristotle's view, fall under the categories of 'where' and 'when,' and because Aristotle recognizes that some terms can be classified under more than one category.[34] However, it is worth observing that a number of later philosophers recognized that the categories of place, time, action and passion, possession, situation, position, are fundamentally relational.[35]

It is worth noting that the relatives of Aristotle's third class, the noetic or, perhaps we should say, the cognitive relations, are described by Aristotle in such a way as to suggest or imply to his medieval interpreters that a relation may be *real* in one of its terms and only *rational* in the other, i.e., that a relation can exist in one thing. We shall find many other reasons in Aristotle's philosophy for regarding relation as attributes of terms taken singly. One of these further reasons is, of course, the necessity in Aristotle's metaphysical doctrines (the point is also made in *De Generatione et Corruptione*, though it does not appear in *Physics* [36]) that the prime mover produce but not undergo motion. This is, as everyone knows, explained by saying that the prime

33. *Ibid.*, 1021ᵃ 27 ff.

34. *Categories*, chap. 8, 11ᵃ 37 ff: "Further, if anything should happen to fall within both the category of quality and that of relation, there would be nothing extraordinary in classing it under both these heads." Cf. Octave Hamelin, *Le Système d'Aristote* (Paris, 1920), p. 106.

35. See Krempel, *La Doctrine de la relation chez St. Thomas*, pp. 432 ff, who quotes Albertus Magnus, Aquinas, Scotus, and Pacius to this effect.

36. See F. Solmsen, *Aristotle's System of the Physical World: A Comparison with his Predecessors* (Ithaca, N.Y., 1961), p. 242.

mover brings about motion in the world as being the object of desire. Such a conception of the ultimate cause is clearly analogous to the cognitive relations, and the plausibility of the idea depends on this analogy. Ultimately, then, one of the roots of Aristotle's treatment of causal relations is his teleological conception of process.

I turn now to the more particular reason why Aristotle treats relations as accidents of one thing at a time. Everything is either a substance (and thus something that can exist separate from other things),[37] or an accident of substance (and thus that which is incapable of separate existence).[38] The way Aristotle states some of these points has to be carefully noticed. "Everything except primary subtances is either predicable of a primary substance or present in a primary substance," [39] and "All things except primary substances are predicable of or present in them, and if primary substance did not exist, it would be impossible for any of the others to exist." [40] It is natural to understand these sentences in the following way: Any attribute is either predicable of a substance or present in a substance. If present in a substance, it is present in one substance at a time. Numerically one accident is, therefore, not in two subjects at a time. It is true that this is not *explicitly* stated. But Aristotle's account of the matter hardly allows another interpretation. The successors of Aristotle, with some hesitation, at least in language, on the part of Simplicius and Al-Farabi, are in general agreement on this point.

Aristotle notices further features of relation. Relations are dependent on other categories, such as quantity, quality, etc.[41] Thus likeness depends on a common quality, equality on the possession

37. *Categories*, chap. 5, 2ᵃ 34 ff, and 2ᵇ 4; *Metaphysics*, Z, 1, 1028ᵃ 34 ff; Λ, 1, 1069ᵃ 25.
38. *Metaphysics*, Z, 1, 1028ᵃ 20 ff; *Physics*, i, 4, 188ᵃ 6; *Categories*, chap. 2, 1ᵃ 20.
39. *Categories*, chap. 5, 2ᵃ 34 ff.
40. *Ibid.*, 2ᵇ 4, trans. R. McKeon, *Basic Writings of Aristotle* (New York, 1941), p. 9.
41. *Metaphysics*, Δ, 15, 1020ᵇ 26–1021ᵃ 35.

of a single common quantity, sameness (here *specific* not numerical identity is intended [42]) on oneness of substance. And this dependence of relations on other categories is the main reason given that relation is the least real of all things.[43] Yet, as one of the categories, relation has *some* reality, since the categories are classifications, not merely of words, but also of features of things.[44]

I have already noticed that for Aristotle some relations are unilateral, i.e., exist in one term without a corresponding relation existing in the other term. This is especially true of the relation of things to the prime mover. But even in the case of causal relations in which both terms of the relation are affected, the description of causal transaction throws some further light on Aristotle's view of relation. In all causal transaction, change is effected by the agent, but occurs *in* the patient. Thus in the *Physics*, the *De Anima*, and the *Metaphysics*, the action of the agent is realized wholly in the patient.[45] The potentialities active and passive are *in* the agent and patient taken severally, and likewise the completed actualizations of agent and patient are, in one sense, *in* the agent and the patient respectively, although in another sense the actualization, as we just saw, is *in* the patient. However causal transaction be interpreted, its foundation as well as its result is in primary substance and not something between two substances. Yet this is not quite correct, either. For the language suggests that, with the exception of the agency of the prime mover, contact between agent and patient is required. The fact is that some of the exigencies of Aristotle's account of the world draw him sometimes in one direction and sometimes in another. A strict adherence to the doctrine that relatives are *in* the related terms

42. Numerical identity is discussed in *De Partibus Animalium*, i, 4, 644ª 24; *Metaphysics*, B, 3, 999ᵇ 33; *Topics*, i, 7, 103ª 6 ff, and vii, 1, 152ª 33–152ᵇ 34; *Physics*, iv, 14, 224ª 1–15; *De Sophisticis Elenchis*, chap. 24, 179ª 37–39.
43. *Metaphysics*, N, 1, 1088ª 15 ff.
44. *Nicomachean Ethics*, i, 6, 1096ª 19 ff; *Metaphysics*, Δ, 7, 1017ª 20 ff, and Θ, 1, 1045ᵇ 32; *De Anima*, i, 5, 410ª 13; cf. *Metaphysics*, Z, 4, 1030ª 17.
45. *Physics*, iii, 3, 202ᵇ 5; *De Anima*, iii, 2, 426ª 4–10; *Metaphysics*, Θ, 8, 1050ª 24 ff.

would lead to a regular-succession view of causal connection, as was the case with Leibniz in his most consistent moments. On the other hand, the necessary character of causal connection can only be elucidated in terms of potentialities which exist in the natures of agent and patient respectively. The requirements of a logical elucidation of the causal nexus are thus in direct conflict with the dynamical view of causation as the actualization of a patient by an agent. The former set of requirements place active and passive powers *in* agents and patients, the latter demand influence passing from the agents to the patients.

Although Aristotle thinks of a relation as a feature of one thing, he always notices, not only that it is a peculiar "pointing" or "referring" feature, but also that relatives must always be understood in terms of their correlative.[46] This suggests a curious point. It is true that relative *terms* are applied to one thing and contain reference to something else. Indeed it is truly predicated of a given thing, a relative *term* must have some extra-cognitive basis (otherwise, the predication would be false). Now, although one substance cannot be contained in another and different substance, some counterpart of the correlative of a thing must exist in that of which it is the correlative if the relative predication is true and if no one accident may exist in more than one subject. It must have been some such line of thought that made it possible for Aristotle to take the view of relations that seems plain in his writings.

There is a passage at the end of *Metaphysics* Zeta which, at first sight, seems to contain a clearer understanding of the nature of relations. This passage, in fact, was used by Duns Scotus as an argument for the extra-mental reality of relations.[47] In this passage, Aristotle argues that in the case of anything which is composed

46. *De Sophisticis Elenchis*, chap. 31, 181ᵇ 26–28; *Topics*, vi, 4, 142ᵃ 28–31, and vi, 8, 146ᵇ 3–4; *Categories*, chap. 7, 8ᵃ 35.
47. Duns Scotus, *Opus Oxoniense*, ii, d. 1, q. 4, n. 7. But see Gregory of Rimini, *Super primum et secundum Sententiarum* (St. Bonaventure, N.Y., 1955; reprint in facsimile of 1522 ed.), i, d. 28, q. 2, fol. 137G, who interprets the passage in its originally intended sense.

(σύνθετον) of something in such a manner that the whole (τὸ πᾶν) is a unit (ἕν) (not as an aggregate is a unit but rather as a syllable is), there must be something besides the constituents. Now this additional feature cannot be another element (στοιχεῖον), for the addition of another element will give us merely a larger aggregate, and this way of attempting to obtain unity will lead to an infinite regression. Thus if we tried to explain how fire and earth constitute flesh, it will not do to add another element in order to account for the composition. We will have fire and earth and the added element, and the problem of explaining the composition will be the same. The additional something, then, cannot be an element, but is the cause why a given matter is flesh and another given matter a syllable, etc. Now this cause or principle (ἀρχή) is not an element but the substance (οὐσία) of each thing.[48] This passage makes it plain that the unity emerging from elements is caused by *form*. Thus it is *form* or *substance* which in Aristotle's thought serves the purpose that other thinkers would assign to relation. It has been suggested to me (by Mr. Gunther Sieburth) that the infinite-regression argument in the passage may well have been directed against the Atomists (especially against Democritus). The infinite-regression argument was later used (perhaps by the Stoics and certainly by some of the Muslim theologians) to refute the reality of relations, and the whole passage was sometimes used to support the extra-mental reality of relations, but Aristotle himself uses it to prove something else, namely, the necessity of form to give unity to several materials.

48. *Metaphysics*, Z, 17, 1041b 11 ff; cf. *ibid.*, H, 6, 1045a 10 ff.

5 · *The Stoics*

A radically nominalistic theory would threaten to remove from relation even this modicum of being. This appears to have occurred in the case of the Stoics. Our knowledge of the Stoic view of relations is quite indirect, but there are enough independent sources to give some idea of the kinds of argument that were used to establish this result. The Stoics rejected Forms. The only reality, is the individual which acts—i.e., an individual body. This radical rejection of everything but individual bodies involved a rejection of universal propositions. Hence the Stoic logic is concerned only with singular and indefinite propositions and with molecular compounds of such propositions. Events or sequence of events are the subject-matter of propositions. Things which happen to individual events, relations, time, space, and the like, are all treated among the "incorporeals," which are described as "the meanings of spoken words," i.e., τὰ λεκτά.[49]

The Stoics admitted four categories: the substratum, quality, condition, and relation. Only the first two are considered as having reality independent of our judgment; the last two depend upon us. The arguments used to establish this subjectivity of relation come to us from Sextus Empiricus, Plotinus, and Simplicius. Since Simplicius depends on Iamblichus, who, in turn, is indebted to Plotinus, we are justified in supposing that Sextus and the Neoplatonists are two independent sources of information. It is worthwhile to examine Sextus' account first.

The Dogmatists (i.e., Stoics, I am sure), says Sextus, describe

---

49. E. Bréhier, *Chrysippe et l'ancien stoïcisme* (Paris, 1951), p. 70, and *La Théorie des incorporels dans l'ancien stoïcisme* (Paris, 1913), p. 20.

the relative as "that which is conceived in relation to another" [50] and this indicates that they regard it as subjective rather than something that exists outside the mind. Again, whatever really exists admits of modification only by being really affected. But relatives can be modified without any such affection; hence they do not really exist. The example given to prove this is so much like those given in Plato's dialogues that it is not improbable that Sextus, or rather, his Stoic source, derived it from that source.[51] If a stick of one cubit is compared to another of one cubit, it is said to be equal to it; if compared with a stick of two cubits, it is no longer equal but unequal; yet it has undergone no internal change. Moreover, one and the same object stands in mutually incompatible relation, so that if relation is real, an absurdity results.

Both Plotinus and Simplicius expound a theory which the latter explicitly identifies as Stoic, according to which the relative is subjective. While the terms referred to by relative expressions exist *ab extra*, the comparison which the relative expression contains comes from us and does not reside in things themselves. *Likeness, right, left,* etc., are all included in this class of subjective conceptions.[52] There is little doubt, then, that the Stoics held a view that relatives are to be regarded as subjective and not as features of the world.[53] The categories of "state" (πῶς ἔχον) and "relation" (πρός τι) are both included by the Stoics among the so-called "incorporeals."

This radically subjective view of relation can be accounted for by the radically nominalistic and materialistic features of Stoic

50. *Adversus Mathematicos*, viii, 453, trans. R. G. Bury, *Sextus Empiricus* (Cambridge, Mass., 1933–1949), II, 475 ff.

51. See *Phaedo*, 102 D; *Theaetetus*, 154 B ff.

52. Plotinus, *Enneads*, vi, 1; Simplicius, *In Categorias*, chap. 7, ed. C. Kalbfleisch, *Commentaria in Aristotelem Graeca*, VIII (Berlin, 1907), 165, ll. 32 ff.

53. There is further support for this interpretation in Proclus, as quoted in *Stoicorum Veterum Fragmenta*, ed. J. von Arnim (Leipzig, 1905–1924), Vol. II, p. 166, no. 521. Cf. Simplicius, *In Categorias*, chap. 7, ed. Kalbfleisch, pp. 165–72.

thought and by the further fact that, for the Stoics, the principle which brings about unity throughout the universe is "the cohesive pneuma of [a] body" and ultimately the pervasive energy which penetrates all things.[54] The Stoic account of causality may also have contributed to this result.[55] In this account, bodies themselves are declared to be the true causes, and events are thought of as both unreal and inefficacious because bodies alone can act and events are only the results of the actions of bodies. However difficult it is to attach any clear meaning to such doctrines, it is historically the origin of the view that was passed on to the Middle Ages, adopted by some, at least, of the orthodox Muslim theologians, and attacked by most of the philosophers of that period.

6 · The Epicureans

It is difficult to discover very much about any specific contribution of the Epicureans to the problem of relation. What little can be extracted from the remains of Epicurus' writings and illuminated by Lucretius (who can generally be taken, in metaphysical questions, as a faithful commentator) is this:

Atoms and space, according to Epicurus, are the only 'separate existents,' that is to say, the only independent realities.[56] The re-

54. See S. Sambursky, *Physics of the Stoics* (London, 1959), p. 118, translated from Achilles, *Isagoge*, 14 (*Stoicorum Veterum Fragmenta*, Vol. II, p. 124, no. 368). Cf. Sextus Empiricus, *Adversus Mathematicos*, ix, 78–80; Galen, *Introductio Scientiae Medicinae*, 9 (*Stoicorum Veterum Fragmenta*, Vol. II, p. 137, no. 416); *De Multitudine*, 3 (*Stoicorum Veterum Fragmenta*, Vol. II, pp. 144–45, no. 439).
55. See Bréhier, *La Théorie des incorporels dans l'ancien stoïcisme*, pp. 17 ff, and his *Chrysippe*, pp. 72–73.
56. Letter to Herodotus, Diogenes Laertius, *Lives of Eminent Philosophers*, x, 40, trans. R. D. Hicks (London, 1925), II, 586, ll. 6 ff.

arrangements of atoms account for change, but in a way that, in one particular, is quite different from that of the earlier Greek Atomists.[57] The characteristics of bodies are either features which always accompany bodies or features which happen to bodies from time to time. The former are inseparable properties (συμβεβηκότα), the latter are accidents (συμπτώματα). Unlike the earlier Atomists, Epicurus insists that sensible accidents do exist, and come into existence as the result of atomic combination and re-arrangements. Some accidents are described as "accidents of accidents"; for example, time is so described.[58] It is plausible to infer from the (incomplete) list of accidents given by Lucretius [59] that relations are to be included among "accidents" (συμπτώματα). But I know of nothing else, in the corpus of Epicurean remains, of importance to our problem. The language, however, suggests that relations are conceived of as accidents of things taken singly, rather than in pairs, triplets, etc.

7 · *The Neoplatonists*

Although the one main problem about relations was communicated to medieval philosophers by Simplicius' *Commentary on the Categories of Aristotle*, the fundamental statement of the problem goes back to Plotinus. In his *Enneads*, vi, 1, Plotinus takes up the Stoic view that relations are fundamentally subjective and attempts to refute it. If the Stoic view were correct, all talk about

57. See, for this, Cyril Bailey, *The Greek Atomists and Epicurus* (Oxford, 1928), pp. 300–309. See also C. J. de Vogel, *Greek Philosophy* (Leiden, 1950–1959), III, 19 ff.

58. Sextus Empiricus, *Adversus Mathematicos*, x, 219; Diogenes Laertius, x, 72; Lucretius, *De Rerum Naturae*, i, 456.

59. *De Rerum Naturae*, i, 455 ff, where slavery, poverty, riches, war and peace (and elsewhere rest and motion) are examples given.

relations would be empty.[60] Again, everyone recognizes that there are relations which he himself does not know about, so that it is impossible to relegate relation to the limbo of consciousness.

The polemic which Plotinus directs against the Stoics plainly depends upon Aristotle's classification and discussion of relations, and, more generally, on the Aristotelian distinctions among the categories. Plotinus' main points in this polemic are, as I have stated, the following: (1) If relational terms have no extra-discussive referents, we are deceived whenever we make relational judgments; i.e., all relational judgments will be false. (2) Whether we state or even conceive that, e.g., one thing is double another or that one thing possesses and another is possessed, in some cases it is nevertheless true that things are so related. Hence relation cannot be regarded as having a merely cognitive status. When we do make comparisons we perceive that relation exists over and above the objects and we notice that the relation is already existent in the object. It is true that, in certain cases, the relation may cease while the objects remain the same, e.g., what was to the right of me is no longer so. Plotinus suggests that this accounts for the notion that relation is not real in such cases.

"Relation" (σχέσις), then, has its own distinctive "actuality" (ὑπόστασις), which is different from the actuality possessed by substance, quantity, or quality. The relations do not give actual existence to their terms; what happens is that when substances, or their qualities or quantities, are compared, it is found that they stand in certain relations which exist in addition to the substances or their qualities or quantities.

The matter which is of primary concern is whether relation is regarded as one characteristic belonging to both terms or whether it is a characteristic of one term with the peculiarity of referring to the other term. Certain passages answer this question beyond much doubt. When he is discussing greatness and smallness in one passage, Plotinus states that these qualities "entail a presence—the

60. *Enneads,* vi, 1, sec. 7.

presence of greatness and smallness respectively," [61] and this is
plainly a repetition of Plato's discussion of these relations in the
Phaedo. Again, in a later passage it is asserted that relative forms
participate in the realm of the unembodied forms, and that, e.g.,
the ideal form of "Doubleness . . . is the cause of a thing being
double." [62] This passage, again, depends on Plato's theory of relational forms in the *Phaedo.*

Enneads, vi, 3, section 28, explicitly states that relation belongs
to one object as compared to another, and that the two objects
enter into the relation together. This statement, which at first sight
looks like an internal contradiction, not to say a contradiction
of other things already stated, can be explained, I think, in the
following way. When one thing becomes the double of another,
the other simultaneously becomes the half of the former, and these
characteristics are respectively characteristics of the two terms
which are mutually interdependent. It does not mean, as I think,
that one characteristic simultaneously belongs to both terms. We
shall find this puzzling sort of statement made over and over again
by later philosophers, such as Albertus Magnus and Aquinas. The
difficulty, in fact, has already been encountered in Plato and Aristotle. All these philosophers notice that a relative can only be
understood as relative in comparison with, or with respect to,
something else. They also notice that correlatives stand in some
kind of interdependence. But the paradigms of substance-attribute
and subject-predicate so dominate their thought, that in the conception of relation they are obliged to ascribe relations to terms
taken severally and singly yet with reference to each other.

It is worth observing that Plotinus also expressly states that
none of the categories may be applied to the "One," and especially notes that He is not related to anything else, since He exists
in Himself and by Himself before the existence of any other
thing.[63] Moreover, when we say that the One is the cause we

61. *Ibid.,* sec. 8 (trans. S. MacKenna [new ed., London, 1956], p. 450).
62. *Ibid.,* sec. 9 (trans. MacKenna, p. 450).
63. *Ibid.,* 8, sec. 11.

are asserting our dependence on the One, for this is to say that we receive something from it even while it exists in itself.[64] This point should be compared with Aristotle's view that the causal relation of the world to God is unilateral. This is a further confirmation of the interpretation of relation as Plotinus sees it.

The fullest discussion of the point already made by Plotinus is to be found in Simplicius. As Martin observed,[65] it was Simplicius who contributed to the medieval world the opposition of the subjectivist treatment of relation and the objectivist views which he and later philosophers defend. In his *Commentary on Aristotle's Categories*, Simplicius states that the Stoics raise the question "whether this connection exists in reality or is only a name applied." [66] Simplicius replies that "either no connection of things exists in reality or some connections exist and others are without reality." This statement must have suggested the distinction between *relatio realis* (a real relation) and *relatio rationis* (a relation produced in the mind without any objective correlate) which plays an important part in medieval discussions.

That we must accept some relations, Simplicius holds, is obvious from the fact that we must assume connections just as we must assume substance, quantity, quality, and the other genera (i.e., categories). If we deny connection we deny the union and harmony of all things. The sciences of geometry and music would be ridiculous if they were concerned with connections that, in fact, do not exist. Moreover, God could hardly be said to be the universal object of desire if what desires it had no connection with it. And again, if there were no connections, priority or posteriority would not exist in objective fact. The multiplicity of things of different sorts can only be explained by connections. A "growing together" of such diverse things is impossible because of their very diversity,

64. *Ibid.*, 9, sec. 3.
65. *Wilhelm von Ockham: Untersuchungen zur Ontologie der Ordnungen*, p. 109.
66. Simplicius, *In Categorias*, chap. 7, ed. Kalbfleisch, p. 169, l. 1. (All translations from Simplicius are by Mr. Gunther Sieburth.)

so that connection alone can constitute the common bond that holds them together.

The language of Simplicius strongly suggests at times that relations are conceived to be between or among the related terms. Yet, when he answers one of the stock objections, viz., that one and the same thing is both greater and smaller, he gives two answers, one of which makes sense only on the supposition that he has adopted the *Phaedo* theory of Plato.[67]

What is fairly conclusive about Simplicius' discussion is that things are said to be related when they participate in a form of connection, and that the definition of this form includes an "inclination toward another." [68] There is an ineradicable vacillation between two ways of viewing relation, or between two aspects of a relational fact. On the one hand, Simplicius writes as though a relation were somehow *between* its terms; on the other hand, he writes as if the participation in a relation-form is the presence of a relational characteristic in one term inclining toward another. The ambiguity of this position will be seen in many medieval authors.

8 · Medieval Views

The discussion of *relation* in medieval Christian thought is complicated by the doctrine that the Persons of the Trinity are constituted by relations and by the doctrine that no accidents can be ascribed to God. These two doctrines require that, while relations among creatures may be treated as accidents, and that relation of creatures to God may be so treated, the relations of the Divine Persons of the Trinity cannot be so regarded without destroying the simplicity and immutability of God. As a conse-

67. *Ibid.*, p. 169.
68. *Ibid.*, p. 175.

quence, although Patristic and Scholastic writers speak of real relations in God, they are not to be regarded as accidents of the divine nature. Hence we always encounter two distinct accounts of relation, namely, one as applied to God and one as applied to creatures.

The main theological doctrines with which medieval discussions of relation are concerned are, therefore, the two following: (1) That the distinction of the Divine Persons must be construed in terms of their mutual relations, and (2) that the relation of a creature to God is, at most, something in the creature only.

Some of the Cappadocian Fathers describe the distinction of the Persons in terms of "relation" (σχέσις). Thus St. Basil asserts that the terms *Father* and *Son* "indicate only a reciprocal relation (τὴν πρὸς ἄλληλα σχέσιν), for the Father is He who granted the principle of existence to another according to a nature similar to His and the Son is he who has received the principle of existence from another by way of generation." [69] But we must turn to St. Augustine for the detailed discussion of this important point. In his *On the Trinity*, Augustine first makes it clear that nothing in God can be said in respect of accident because there can be no accidents in God. But on the other hand, not everything assertable of God can be said solely with respect to the divine substance. The only category applicable to God other than substance is, accordingly, relation. For the Father is so called only in relation to His eternal Son, and likewise, the latter only in relation to the former. If the generation of the Son were temporal it might be said to be an accident, but as it is an eternal generation, it can only be characterized in terms of relation. And the relation in this case is not accident precisely because it is not changeable but rather eternal.[70]

Augustine makes a further point worthy of notice. In all cases, not only is there a difference between absolute and relative terms,

69. *Adversus Eunomium*, ii, 22 (ed. J. P. Migne, *Patrologiae Graecae* [Paris, 1845–1866], Vol. XXIX, col. 621), cited in H. A. Wolfson, *The Philosophy of the Church Fathers* (Cambridge, Mass., 1956), I, 341.
70. *De Trinitate*, v, chap. 5, no. 6.

but any native or essence which is said to be "in relation" still remains something even when its relative rôle is taken away.[71] That is to say that the relative characterization of anything presupposes that there is a substantial foundation which is real and quite independent of the relation.

The relation of God to His creatures is explained in a way that was to become traditional and orthodox. When something is said of God relative to the creature, this implies a real accident in the creature but not in God. Thus anything which is said of God in time, yet which was not said of Him before, is clearly to be regarded as said of Him relatively. But this is not so on account of any accident in God, in the sense that anything may have happened to Him; rather it is only according to that in respect of which God begins to be called something relatively.[72] Because God is unchangeable, He neither has nor can acquire any accident. Hence relative terms applied to God in relation to creatures at most refer to relative accidents of the creatures. This resolution of the problem resembles that of Aristotle with respect to the prime mover, and is a further confirmation of the doctrine that a relation is in one of its terms as an accident.

The commentaries of Boethius make occasional reference to relations, but it is to his tract *On the Trinity* that we must turn to discover further elaboration of the theme that the Persons of the Trinity are distinguished by their relations. Although this tract is much quoted in medieval philosophical and theological discussions, the doctrine lends itself to as wide a series of interpretations as possible. In some statements of Boethius, relation is explicitly decribed as something external to the nature of a thing.[73] In the tract *On the Trinity*, relation is described as that which established the distinction of the Persons. But it is explicitly denied that the relations of the Persons are accidents, on the ground that accidents are transient, whereas no changes of any kind can occur

71. *Ibid.*, vii, chap. 1, no. 2.
72. *Ibid.*, v, chap. 16, no. 17.
73. Boethius, *De Trinitate*, v.

in the Godhead. Thus Boethius contributes to the pattern of elucidation that was to be followed in the Middle Ages: relations in creatures are accidents, relations of the Divine Persons are not accidents.

Johannes Scotus Eriugena does not add much to the elucidation of the problem. Although he insisted that none of the categories is applicable, literally, to the super-essential God, we can use categorical terms of God in a superlative sense. A fortiori, we can apply "relation" (*habitudo*) in a superlative sense to the Divine Persons.[74] Eriugena's notion of the superlative sense, derived from Pseudo-Dionysius and ultimately from the Neoplatonic doctrine that we cannot know the divine nature, makes it impossible to say to what extent the problem of relations in the Godhead is elucidated. When he speaks of relations of creatures he insists that relation involves two things and that it is an accident.[75]

The main result of these earlier speculations is this: relations of creatures are treated as accidents, while relations in the Godhead cannot be so treated. We shall see later what was done with this by theologians and philosophers in the twelfth and succeeding centuries of the medieval period. But it is necessary first of all to discuss some of the doctrines about relation among the Muslim philosophers, because the interesting doctrines of the thirteenth and fourteenth centuries cannot be understood without taking into account the views of Avicenna, and his views cannot be understood without understanding the views of the Mutakallimun.

A group of orthodox theologians in medieval Islam, the Mutakallimun, held an extremely radical view about relations. The origin of this group of theologians is rather obscure but the general outline of their program is somewhat as follows: In the interests of Muslim orthodoxy they defended an atomistic theory which, although it doubtless owes something to Greek atomism and perhaps also to Indian atomistic theories, has unique features

---

74. Johannes Scotus Eriugena, *De Divisione Naturae*, i, 13 (ed. J. P. Migne, *Patrologia Latina*, Vol. CXXII, cols. 456–58).
75. *Ibid.*, i, 19–24 (*P.L.*, Vol. CXXII, cols. 466–70).

of its own. The omnipotence of God requires an absolute inefficacy of creatures, i.e., God is the only genuine cause in the universe. This view was defended in a number of ways. According to the account in Maimonides, the followers of this school maintained that whatever was conceivable by the imagination is to be admitted as possible.[76] What this means is that whatever involves no logical absurdity can occur if God wishes that it occur.[77] Therefore there can be no proof of causal connection in the world. The physical world, in fact, consists of atoms which, together with their accidents, are continuously re-created. This is simply the most radical form of the doctrine of divine conservation.

Although some members of this group of theologians admitted the existence of accidents, indeed, accidents of unusual kinds (e.g., the accident of extinction which God creates when He wishes to annihilate atoms), they appear to have regarded relations as being purely subjective. One of the favorite arguments against relatives used by the Mutakallimun is the infinite regress which is supposed to follow from admitting objective relational accidents. As stated by Fakhr al-Din al-Razi (d. 1209 and a late source but on this point presumably reliable) the argument runs as follows:

If a relational accident were real it would have to inhere in a substratum. But this inherence would be another relation between the essence of the first relation and the substrate. Moreover, it would be different from the essence of the relation, and this different reality would also have to exist in a substratum. Now *this* inherence-relation (of second order) is added to the essence, and must inhere in its turn, so that there results an infinite chain of inherence-relations.[78]

76. Maimonides, *Guide for the Perplexed*, Part I, chap. 73, 10th Proposition (trans. by M. Friedländer [London, 1928], pp. 127–28).

77. *Ibid.* Cf. Al-Ghazali, *Tahafut al-Falasifah*, in Averroes' *Tahafut al-Tahafut*, trans. by S. van den Bergh (London, 1954), I, 316 ff.

78. Fakhr al-Din al-Razi, in Max Horten, *Die Philosophischen Systeme der Spekulativen Theologen im Islam* (Bonn, 1912), pp. 8 ff. Cf. Averroes, *Tahafut al-Tahafut*, trans. van den Bergh, *passim*. See also I. Madkour,

Furthermore God is simultaneous with everything temporal, and so, if relations were objective realities, the changes and generation and corruption of temporal things would involve changes in God, which is impossible. This motive for denying objective reality to relations is encountered throughout medieval thought. (Sometimes, however, it is employed to prove that some relations, while real, have existence in only one term of the relation.)

The main treatise on the problem of the reality of relations which influenced the discussions in medieval Christendom is to be found in Avicenna's *Metaphysics*. We know from the *Fihrist* (tenth century) that Simplicius' *Commentary on the Fourth Book of Aristotle's Categories* (on relatives) existed in an Arabic translation. It is, therefore, reasonable to suppose that Avicenna's discussion is based, in part, on the views of the Mutakallimun and on Simplicius' commentary. Avicenna's discussion must be seen, then, as a reply to those who denied the objectivity of relations, i.e., the Stoics as reported by Simplicius and the Mutakallimun.

Avicenna's discussion in his *Metaphysics* begins with the assertion that there is no doubt that, considered as a real existent, relation is an accident. For relation cannot be apprehended as something existing in itself (i.e., a substance). Thus Avicenna appears to depend here on the assumption that whatever exists is either substance or accident. Hence a relation can be conceived only as inhering in one thing and pointing toward another.

But relations, as accidents, differ. Some are of the sort that the relation is different in the two terms; others are of the sort that the relation is similar in the two terms. Of the first sort there are, e.g., *the double* and *the half;* of the second, *equal magnitude* to *equal magnitude, touching* and *touching,* etc. It is clear from what is said here and later that Avicenna means the following: There are two accidents involved in many (although, as will be made clear presently, not in all) relations. In the case of asymmetrical relations, the relational accident of one of the terms is of a differ-

---

L'Organon d'Aristote dans le monde Arabe (Paris, 1934), p. 87, and the references cited there.

ent kind from the relational accident of the other term. But there is no single (numerically one) reality which exists in both terms of any relation. Thus the relational accident "fatherhood" exists in the father (albeit only with reference to the child) and the relational accident of "sonship" exists only in the child (albeit only with reference to the father). We have no acquaintance with, or name for, a reality which is, so to speak, a substrate for both fatherhood and sonship. Similar considerations hold with respect to symmetrical relation, e.g., the relation of fraternity (more exactly, "siblinghood"). Although the relational accident of one sibling is specifically the same as that of the other, there are two numerically different accidents involved, one inhering in one of the siblings, the other inhering in the other. The same holds of other symmetrical relations, e.g., the relation of contact between two contiguous things—one has "a contact" with respect to the other, and the other has "a contact" with respect to the one, but these are two numerically distinct accidents. "Do not believe," Avicenna insists at this point, "that numerically one and the same accident may exist in two substrates." [79]

There are relations which are unilateral, i.e., where there is a relational accident existing in only one term. This happens in the cases of knowing and the known (here, knowing exists in the knower but there is no corresponding relational accident in what is known).

Avicenna, as was mentioned before, had read of the Stoic doctrine that relations are purely subjective and was unquestionably acquainted with the same thesis in the writings of the Mutakallimun. He finds it necessary, therefore, to defend the objective reality of relations. He mentions sympathetically the argument

79. The main discussion of Avicenna is in *Metaphysica*, tract iii, chap. 10 (*Metaphysica sive Prima Philosophia* [Venice, 1495; reprinted Louvain, 1961]). I have used the following works for this account of Avicenna: Max Horten, *Die Metaphysik Avicennas* (Halle, 1907), pp. 230 ff; M. M. Anawati, *Ibn Sina: La Métaphysique du Shifā'* (Quebec, 1952), Fascicule 1, pp. 99–104. The translation is my own, made directly from the Latin text except where Horten and Anawati indicate a fuller expression.

that relations are objectively real because, e.g., some person is father of another whether or not anyone perceives or understands that this is the case. (This argument occurs in Simplicius and his sources, especially Plotinus.) Then he deals with the infinite-regress argument against the reality of relation, which, as we have seen, was one of the main arguments of the Mutakallimun. His answer is very difficult to follow but it amounts, as far as I can see, to the assertion that the relational accident, by its nature, relates without any need of further relational accidents. These further 'relations' are purely conceptual and have intra-mental existence merely. It is not clear to me that Avicenna has succeeded in answering the Mutakallimun.

The important features of Avicenna's doctrine about relation seem to be as follows: Relations are objectively real. But, as they are not substantival realities, they must be accidents.[80] And, although relational accidents have the peculiarity that they inhere in one subject 'with respect to another,' as numerically single accidents they exist in only one subject. Thus the idea that one relation inheres in both terms is explicitly repudiated. There are relations which are 'bi-lateral,' i.e., where a relational accident exists in one term and a corresponding relational accident exists in the other term. Some relations, however, are 'unilateral,' i.e., a relational accident exists in only one of the terms. It is clear that the notion of a 'unilateral' relation is possible only if a relation is treated as a special kind of accident. The importance of this for theology has already been mentioned in the case of Aristotle, and we shall encounter it again.

Moses Maimonides remarks, in his *Guide for the Perplexed*, that relations are not the essence of a thing and that they are not so intimately connected with it as are qualities. He further observes that there are no relations between God and creatures, for other-

80. It is worth noticing that, elsewhere in the *Metaphysics*, Avicenna repeats Aristotle's critique of the Platonists, viz., that they made something accidental, namely 'The great and the small,' basic to substantival realities.

wise God would be subject to the accident of relation.[81] This
suggests both that Maimonides thinks of relation as an accident
and also that his denial of accidents in God is in accord with the
prevailing opinion on the subject.

The views of Averroes on the subject of relations are not always verbally consistent with one another.[82] But some of his
explicit statements on the subject are repeated in several works
and appear to represent a considered opinion. In his *Epitome of
Metaphysics,* he stated that "this category [sc. of relation] is
something which the soul introduces into existing things. If there
were no soul, there would also be no relations . . . ." [83] In the
Great Commentary on the Metaphysics he states that some people,
having noticed that *relation* has the least stability of all the categories, decided that *relation* should not be included among the
categories but rather among the predicables.[84] For the predicables
(*definition, genus,* etc.) are 'second intention,' whereas the concepts comprised under the several categories are first intentions.
In his *Tahafut al-Tahafut* he explicitly stated that "not all the different dispositions which can be imagined in a thing need determine additional qualities in its essence outside the soul; indeed,
this is the case with the disposition of privations and relations, and
for this reason certain philosophers do not count the category of
relation among things which exist outside the soul, i.e. the ten
categories." [85]

This passage, taken by itself, might simply mean that *some* items
falling under the category of relations are purely beings of reason
(*entia rationis*). But when it is compared with other passages it
appears to mean that *all* relations are intra-mental merely. Krempel
holds that passages can be found which support (1) the subjec-

81. *Guide for the Perplexed,* Part I, chap. 52 (trans. Friedländer, p. 71).
82. See Max Horten, *Die Metaphysik des Averroes* (Halle, 1912), pp. x–xi.
83. See *Die Epitome der Metaphysik des Averroes,* trans. S. van den Bergh
(Leiden, 1924), p. 70.
84. *In Metaphysicam,* xii, text 19 (*Opera Omnia Aristotelis* [Venice, 1574],
VIII, 144ʳ).
85. Averroes, *Tahafut al-Tahafut,* trans. S. van den Bergh, I, 119, ll. 8–13.

tivity, (2) the objectivity, and (3) the transcendental character of relation, and cites in support of the third doctrine the following passage from the *Epitome of the Metaphysics:* "Fire *qua* fire, belongs to the category of substance; but fire *qua* cause belongs to the category of relation." He explains the meaning of this view thus: Everything is both an absolute and a relative thing, though a relation is not something really distinct from permanent beings.[86] It is, therefore, not possible to determine with any accuracy at present what Averroes' view was, or whether he had a consistent view on the subject. However, his views were often quoted by the Christian Scholastics and for this reason must be included in our consideration.

According to Aquinas, relations are of several sorts: Some are merely ideal in both terms, some are real in both terms, and some are ideal in one term but real in the other. Some 'relations' do not have any counterpart in the nature of things but exist only in the mind. From Aristotle and Avicenna we can discover that this happens in four different ways:

1. When something is referred to itself (e.g., when we relate the same to the same). If the relation of self-identity had an extra-cognitive counterpart, there would be an infinite regress because the relation of identity would be objectively identical with itself through another objectively real relation of identity, etc., *ad infinitum.*

2. When a relation itself is related to something. For if the relation of a relation to its subject were objectively real we would encounter another infinite regress. (This is the argument of the Mutakallimun which Avicenna tries to meet in *Metaphysica,* tract iii, chap. 10.) Hence the relation of a relation to its subject is a *relatio rationis tantum.*

3. When one of the relatives is dependent on the other but not conversely, the relation is real in the dependent term but rational merely in the term on which the other term depends. This holds

86. Krempel, *La Doctrine de la relation chez St. Thomas,* pp. 492–93.

(*a*) in the case of knowledge and an object known, when the relation is real in the knower but merely a *relatio rationis* in the object known; (*b*) in the case of the relation of God to creatures.

4. When that which now exists is compared with that which does not exist, as when we say that things existing now are prior to things existing in the future. For this would, possibly, involve an infinite progression if there were to be generation in the future *in infinitum.*[87]

Several causes contribute to the view that relations are not extra-cognitively real. One is that, in fact, some relations are merely *entia rationis*. Another is that relation is the least real of beings, since it is in some way dependent on other accidents of the substance in which it inheres, and since it depends on another thing to which it is referred.[88] Still another cause is the fact that relations are more difficult to cognize than other accidents because a relation is not a *sensible* accident (although its cause can be sensible accidents).[89]

For all these causes, some philosophers have denied the reality of relations altogether. But this view is mistaken, because there is evidently order and relationship in the universe.[90] This order is exhibited chiefly in the teleological relations which the parts of given things have to the whole thing, which various things have to one another, and which everything in the universe has to God.[91] Hence some relations are objectively real.

The nature of these real relations must now be ascertained. In creatures, relations are accidents,[92] and as accidents, are certain

---

87. *De Veritate*, q. 1, a. 5, ad 7[um]; *Summa Theologiae*, Part I, q. 13, a. 7.
88. *Summa contra Gentiles*, iv, 14, [par. 12].
89. *Sententiarum*, iv, d. 27, q. 1, a. 1; cf. *In X Libros Ethicorum*, i, lectio 1; *Summa Theologiae*, Part II, q. 58 a. 4.
90. *Summa Theologiae*, Part I, q. 13, a. 7—the basic response of Plotinus, Simplicius, Avicenna, et al. to the radically subjectivist doctrines of Stoics and Mutakallimun.
91. *Ibid.*, q. 65, a. 2.
92. *Quaestiones de Quolibet*, i, a. 2; *Summa Theologiae*, Part I, q. 28, a. 1 and a. 2.

forms inhering in substances.[93] In fact, the *being* of a relation, like the being of any accident, depends on the being in which it inheres.[94] And the main reason why a relation must be an accident is that everything real is either substance or accident, and since relations are not substances, they must be accidents.[95]

Now the accidental character of relations suggests a problem. No accident can exist in two different subjects.[96] Yet a relation is "to something" (*ad aliquid*) and thus in some way depends on something other than the subject in which it inheres. Aquinas resolves this difficulty by stating that "a relation according to its *being* insofar as it has a foundation in a thing is an *extreme* but insofar as it is a relation it is a *mean*." [97] Its nature (*ratio*) is to be "to something," whereas its existence depends on the subject in which it inheres.[98] This resolution of the difficulty had been, in principle, already stated by Albertus Magnus.[99]

Thus real relations, in contrast to relations of mere reason, are accidents. In some cases, however, the relation is real in one term and merely rational in the other term. This, as we have already seen, holds in the cases of (1) knower and known (where knowledge in the knower is a real modification of the knower but in no wise affects the object known), (2) in relations between

93. *Summa contra Gentiles*, iv, 14; *Compendium Theologiae*, i, 90.

94. *De Principiis Naturae*, chap. 1 (see *Opuscula Philosophica S. Thomae Aquinatis* [Rome, 1954], p. 121).

95. *Summa Theologiae*, Part I, q. 76, a. 6, ad 4um; *De Potentia Dei*, q. 8, a. 2.

96. *Sententiarum*, i, d. 27, q. 1, a. 1, ad 2um.

97. *De Potentia Dei*, q. 8, a. 2.

98. *Sententiarum*, ii, d. 40, q. 1, a. 4, ad 1um; *ibid.*, i, d. 27, q. 1, a. 1, ad 2um; *ibid.*, iii, d. 18, q. 1, ad 4um. Cf. Avicenna, *Metaphysica*, tract iii, chap. 10; Albertus Magnus, *Liber de Praedicamentis*, tract iv, chap. 10; Fakhr al-Din al-Razi (in Horten, *Die Philosophischen Systeme der Spekulativen Theologen im Islam*, p. 9); F. Suarez, *Disputationes Metaphysicae*, Disputatio XLVII, sec. 6, no. 4; Leibniz, *Die Philosophischen Schriften von G. W. Leibniz*, ed. C. J. Gerhardt (Berlin, 1875–1890), II, 486 and 457; also Leibniz's *New Essays*, Book II, chap. 12, sec. 7, and *5th Paper to Clarke*, sec. 42.

99. Albertus Magnus, *Liber de Praedicamentis*, tract iv (*Opera Omnia*, ed. A. Borgnet [Paris, 1890–1899], I, 241); *Summa Theologica*, i, tract ix, q. 39, membr. 1, ad 2um, loco 2 (*Opera Omnia*, ed. Borgnet, XXXI, 395).

what exists and what does not exist (for there can be no real relational accident in a non-existent), (3) God and creatures (creation is an accident in creatures but there is no corresponding accident in God). This last case deserves further discussion.

The Aristotelian doctrine that God moves the world as being the object of the world's desire was, as I have already noticed, required by the fact that God, as pure form, is free from mutability of any kind. This much of Aristotle was adopted by many of the Christian Scholastics and, in particular, by Aquinas. The teleological explanation of causal connection ultimately in terms of the tendency, desire, or inclination of things to imitate God made this account of ultimate causality plausible. It is clear, then, that the present account of relations as accidents is the only one that is consistent with the Aristotelian and Thomist view of the nature of God and His causal action.

Not every case of causal relations can be dealt with so simply, because in the causal relations of finite agents and their patients there is a modification of both agent and patient. And as Krempel has noticed, there are apparently conflicting texts which must be considered. In some places, Aquinas asserts that the action of an agent is realized only in the patient.[100] But in other texts we are told that action is in the agent as an accident in a subject.[101] Krempel suggests the following solution of the apparent inconsistency of these texts: "The solution is revealed by the distinction, in all genuine change, of a *two-fold* process: one in the interior of the passive subject, . . . the other [a process] *from the active subject to the passive subject.*" [102] The first group of texts are concerned with the former process, the second with the latter process. And in fact Aquinas states that "in every genuine muta-

---

100. Aquinas, *In De Anima,* iii, lectio 2; *In VIII Libros Physicorum,* iii, lectio 4, etc. These views depend on Aristotle, *De Anima,* iii, 2, 426ᵃ 9; *Physics,* iii, 3, 202ᵇ 5; *Metaphysics,* Θ, 8, 1050ᵃ 24 ff.

101. *Summa contra Gentiles,* ii, 9; *De Potentia Dei,* q. 8, a. 2; *Sententiarum,* ii, d. 40, q. 1, a. 1.

102. Krempel, *La Doctrine de la relation chez St. Thomas,* p. 444.

tion and motion a two-fold process is discovered: *one* from one term of motion to another as from whiteness to blackness [in a given subject]; *another* from agent to patient, as from one making to what is made." [103]

The question remains, however, how the relation of agent to patient is to be conceived. Aquinas insists that action is a passing-over from agent to patient, or genuinely a mean (*media*) between agent and the subject receiving action.[104] Yet he is no less insistent that agency does not consist in the passage of any thing or accident from one thing to another. An accident in one subject can produce a numerically distinct but specifically identical accident in another subject. But this amounts to the agent's eliciting an accident in the patient from potency to act.[105] However, what the *influence* of agent on patient actually is remains mysterious.[106] In fact, the chief themes in this view of causality and relation appear to be in conflict with one another. For, in order to obtain necessary connection [107] between agent and patient and in order to explain the unilateral relation of divine causality, relations have to be treated as accidents. But in order to classify a causal nexus *between* agent and patient, another and radically different view of relations would seem to be required. It is possible, of course, to hold that causal *influence* is something distinct from and prior to the relational accidents in patient and agent which result from this *influence*.[108] But what this influence is and how it fits into the scheme of a world in which everything is either substance or accident remains obscure.

Aquinas felt compelled to take the view that some relations are objectively real for other reasons which have not yet been mentioned. Aristotle would certainly not have included relations

103. *De Potentia Dei*, q. 3, a. 3.
104. *Summa Theologiae*, Part I, q. 54, a. 1, ad 3[um]; *ibid.*, q. 56, a. 1.
105. *De Potentia Dei*, q. 3, a. 7; *Summa contra Gentiles*, iii, 69.
106. See Krempel, *La Doctrine de la relation chez St. Thomas*, p. 446.
107. *De Potentia Dei*, q. 3, a. 17, ad 4[um]; *In XII Libros Metaphysicorum*, v, lectio 3; *Summa Theologiae*, Part I, q. 19, a. 3, ad 6[um].
108. Suarez, *Disputationes Metaphysicae*, Disputatio XII, sec. 2, no. 13.

among the categories if they were not objectively real. Simplicius, Avicenna, and others reinforced this by further consideration, and Aquinas shows that he has read these arguments.[109] Also the Council of Reims in 1148 had reinforced the views of Augustine and Boethius (the official doctrine of the Church for a long time [110]) in declaring for real relations among the Persons of the Trinity. But in addition to authorities secular and sacred, Aquinas was convinced that the completeness and goodness of the world is exhibited by the connections of things which exist independently of and prior to our cognitions.[111]

The relations in God by which the Divine Persons are distinguished are not accidents, because there are no accidents in God. They are, therefore, the same with the divine substance itself. Nonetheless, Aquinas maintains that these relations in God are real and not merely consequences of our understanding.[112]

There are, of course, relations which are merely the result of our understanding and which have, therefore, no objective counterpart. But the relations which are real are objective features of those things of which they are asserted. These real relations are accidents which belong to one substance insofar as their existence is concerned but which are "to another" so far as their nature goes. Hence we find Aquinas struggling toward a satisfactory view of relations but failing to achieve it for the reasons indicated. The demands of theology, the dominance of the substance-accident ontology, and other causes prevented him from achieving a completely satisfactory doctrine. We shall find that his successors fared little better.

The views of Scotus cannot be completely understood without a detailed analysis of the doctrines of Henry of Ghent. But, as

---

109. *De Potentia Dei*, q. 7, a. 9; *Sententiarum*, i, d. 26, q. 2, a. 1.

110. See H. Denzinger, *Enchiridion Symbolorum* (Freiburg, 1910), nos. 278, 280, on the Eleventh Council of Toledo; no. 428 on the Fourth Lateran Council. And see H.-F. Dondaine, O.P., trans., *Somme Théologique, Saint Thomas d'Aquin, La Trinité* (2nd ed., Paris, 1950), I, 232 ff.

111. *De Potentia Dei*, q. 7, a. 9.

112. *Summa Theologiae*, Part I, q. 28, a. 1.

against Henry of Ghent, who had argued that a relation is merely a 'mode' of the being of a substance, Scotus insists that relatives are real accidents which (with some exceptions to be noted) are really different from the substances in which they inhere.[113]

Against Henry of Ghent, Scotus argues that, as there are many relations the foundation of which can exist in the absence of the relation without contradiction, there are many relations which are not really identical with their foundations. For instance, this white thing can exist without similarity. If another white thing comes into being, then similarity begins to exist in this white thing. Hence, the foundation of the relation can exist without the relation. The same holds true of asymmetrical relations: a man can begin as not being a master and then acquire power over someone, thus acquiring the relation of mastership.[114]

Scotus shows the influence of Simplicius' discussion in many ways. He quotes him in the discussion of the reality of relations. He also is dependent on Avicenna's treatment of the subject, for he introduces the infinite-regress argument. Aristotle's use of this argument against the Atomists is also used in this connection. As Scotus puts the argument, it runs somewhat as follows:

If a relation were something other than its foundation, there would be a process to infinity in relations. For if a relation were other than its foundation, by the same token this "otherness" (*alietas*), which is a kind of relation, is also other than its foundation, and thus there will be an infinite process in relations. He refutes this and other arguments purporting to identify relations with their foundations. The most important argument he uses is as follows: If A and B compose the composite AB and the union of these parts is nothing but the absolute terms A and B, then if A and B are actually separated, the whole reality of A and B

---

113. See Martin, *Wilhelm von Ockham: Untersuchungen zur Ontologie der Ordnungen,* pp. 120 ff. We should especially notice that the 'real difference' which Scotus has in mind here is not precisely the 'real difference' of Ockham which we shall discuss later.

114. *Opus Oxoniense,* ii, d. 1, q. 4, no. 11.

(considered as united) remains, so that A and B separated remain really united. The unity of A and B taken together would be merely a unity of aggregation, and thus the hypothesis of a real union of parts is contradicted.

Another argument is derived from a consideration of causation. Whatever is caused by diverse second causes requires that these causes be approximated to the object in which the effect is to be produced. Now if this approximation and proposition of the causative elements in the situation were merely the absolute terms themselves, these absolute terms will be causative even when they are not approximated. A relation, then, cannot be identical with its foundation.

The opinion that a relation is merely a being of reason (*ens rationis*) is equally defective. For if all relations were merely beings of reason, the unity of the universe, which consists in the mutual order of its parts and the order of each thing to the First Being, would be destroyed. Moreover, a real union of parts cannot consist of a mere reason (*ratio*) caused by the mind of the beholder. Moreover, as all secondary causes operate by approximation, this approximation cannot be a mere being of reason, for if it were, there would be no causation. Moreover, the denial of the extra-cognitive reality of relations would destroy mathematics, which is full of demonstrations of the relations of things.

However, not all real relations are *really distinct* from their foundations.[115] For that which exists in a thing in such a way that

115. This expression "really distinct" requires elucidation here because it is essential in Duns Scotus and William of Ockham. As Scotus uses the term 'distinction,' an unqualifiedly real distinction between two things requires their separation or separability. A formal distinction, on the other hand (Scotus sometimes calls this distinction "a formal non-identity," especially when speaking of the Divine Persons), is a distinction or formal non-identity which exists objectively, i.e., prior to any act of an intellect human or divine, in the thing, but which admits of no separation, not even a separation effected by divine power. In the present case, an accident has its own proper being and is thus really distinct from its subject in the following senses: (1) absolute accidents can exist without a subject (as in the case of the consecrated Host), and substances can exist without their accidents,

the thing cannot, consistently, exist without it is really identical with that thing. Now the relation of any creature (e.g., a stone) to God is *in* the creature in such a way that the creature cannot exist without this relation. It follows that the relation in question is *really* the same as the thing. Yet it is *formally* distinct from the creature in the sense that the relation is not "adequately identical" with its relation to God. Thus the relation of creature to God is *formally* distinct from, but really identical with, the creature.[116] That this is the view of Duns Scotus is confirmed by William of Ockham, who explicitly tells us that according to Scotus "some relations are really distinguished, and some are not really distinguished." [117]

It is worth noting that Duns Scotus also employs his "formal distinction" to elucidate the distinction of the Persons of the Trinity, so that their distinction by their relations is a formal distinction, but, in no sense of course, a distinction of accidents.

The theory of relation in William of Ockham is very difficult to elucidate for several reasons, of which the most important is the following. On the one hand, Ockham distinguishes between real relations and relations of reason.[118] On the other hand, Ockham holds that relations are only concepts or "intentions" in the soul, involving a plurality of things.[119] At first sight these two are so plainly incompatible that it would seem impossible to get any consistent doctrine. But, although Ockham's doctrine of relations is by no means free of difficulty, we shall see how he can consistently maintain that there is a basis for the distinction be-

---

whether relative accidents or absolute accidents; (2) relative accidents cannot exist apart from their *foundation* and *terms,* but the foundation or terms can exist without the relative accidents. In this sense, relative accidents are *really distinct* from their subjects.

116. *Opus Oxoniense,* ii, d. 1, q. 5.

117. William of Ockham, *Sententiarum,* ii, q. 2, E (*Opera Plurima* [Lyon, 1494–1496], reprinted in facsimile [London, 1962], Vol. IV); cf. Martin, *Wilhelm von Ockham: Untersuchungen zur Ontologie der Ordnungen,* pp. 120 ff.

118. *Sententiarum,* i, d. 30, q. 5, F–H.

119. *Ibid.,* q. 1, R.

tween real and merely rational relations and, at the same time, maintain that relations are only concepts.

We can see Ockham's views on relation most clearly in terms of the views which he was opposing. There is some evidence that the first book of the *Questions on the Sentences* (or, more correctly, the *Ordinatio*, in contrast to the remaining three books, which are *Reportationes*) contains Ockham's earliest treatment of the subject.[120] Here, as a comparison of texts reveals, the first question is an attempt to refute the views of Duns Scotus.[121] Here Ockham asks "whether, if we exclude the authority of faith and of philosophers, it is easier to deny that a relation *from the side of the thing* [i.e., as *we* would say, 'objectively speaking'] is a thing distinct from an absolute or from absolutes in any way than to affirm such a proposition." [122] Ockham defends the doctrine that, objectively speaking, a relation is not something distinct from one or more absolute things. By 'absolute things' Ockham means individual substances and individual qualities. That qualities are absolute things in addition to substances is maintained for the reason, among others, that God can without contradiction create and conserve accidents without substances just as He can create and conserve substances without accidents.[123] But it is true, even within the frame of natural reason, that substance and accident are of different natures and so can be conceived independently, so that the conception of a substance or the conception of an accident is an absolute term (i.e., a term which does not require reference to something other than the principal referent in order to be understood).[124]

What Ockham is denying, then, is that relations exist in the

---

120. See *ibid.*, qq. 1–5.
121. As expressed, especially, in *Opus Oxoniense*, ii, d. 1, qq. 4–5.
122. *Sententiarum*, i, d. 30, q. 1.
123. *Ibid.*, ii, q. 5, M; *De Sacramento Altaris*, chap. 12.
124. In his *Summa Logicae*, Part I, chap. 53, Ockham says that it is terms, rather than things, that are properly called *absolute* or *relative*. Cf. *Quodlibeta Septem*, vi, q. 16. But in the *Sententiarum* he nevertheless speaks of *absolute things*.

nature of things outside our consciousness, in addition to substances and qualities. Now, as his opponents, for the greater part if not entirely, maintained that there are relative accidents, Ockham must be understood to deny that any such relative accidents exist in the nature of things.

Relations, for Ockham, are concepts or intentions of the mind which differ from other concepts in the following way. Whereas the concept of *substance* or *absolute accident* refers to individuals taken one at a time, a relational concept refers to individuals taken two or more at a time and taken conjunctively.[125] Now this is Ockham's distinctive contribution to the medieval discussions of relation. He refuses to identify a relation with its foundation (a view sometimes attributed to Henry of Ghent), because a relation, for Ockham, is an intention in the soul. But he equally insists that some relations, namely real relations, have a basis in the nature of things existing outside of, and independent of, consciousness. In fact, we can say that the *similarity* of two men, say Socrates and Plato, is simply *Socrates and Plato*.[126] But the similarity is not something distinct from the two (or more) resembling things taken as accidents of those things. These two statements, viz., (1) that a relation is not identical with its foundation and (2) that it is not an external reality distinct from its terms, may seem to be incompatible. For Ockham they are not, because, in denying that a relation is identical with its foundation, he implies that a relation is not a determination of one thing only, but rather of at least two things.[127] And in denying that a relation is distinct from its two (or more) terms, he implies that there is no relational

125. *Sententiarum*, i, d. 30, q. 1, R: "dico quod relatio non est fundamentum sed tantum intentio et conceptus in anima importans plura absoluta"; cf. *ibid.*, q. 2, L, and *ibid.*, q. 4, E; *Quodlibeta Septem*, vi, q. 15; *Expositio super Physicam Aristotelis* (Berlin, cod. elect. 974), fols. 97ᵈ, 126ᵃ, 177 (see entry under 'relatio' in L. Baudry, *Lexique Philosophique de Guillaume d'Ockham* [Paris, 1958], p. 232).

126. *Sententiarum*, i, d. 30, q. 5; cf. q. 3.

127. See Martin, *Wilhelm von Ockham: Untersuchungen zur Ontologie der Ordnungen*, p. 145.

accident inhering in either or both of the terms. Those of Ockham's predecessors who had treated relations as accidents had supposed that such accidents inhere in each of the related terms.[128] Simplicius is exceptional, as Martin has observed,[129] in suggesting that a relation is, in some way, in both of its terms, and, even here, it is far from clear that Simplicius actually intended this as a "ligament" joining distinct things, although Ockham understood Simplicius in this way.[130]

Again, there seems to be a discrepancy between Ockham's statement that a relation is an intention in the mind involving two or more things taken together and his statement that a relation is its terms together. This discrepancy, I think, cannot be so easily explained away. Thus we cannot say *both* that similarity is an intention or concept *of* two (or more) resembling things and that similarity *is* two (or more) resembling things.

But, neglecting these difficulties, Ockham's main contribution is that relational concepts signify many things (i.e., two or more) taken conjunctively. This seems to be sound, or at least, a more correct view than the prevailing doctrine that relational concepts refer to peculiar referring accidents inhering in one term and depending in some way also upon the other term to which the accident inhering in the one term refers.

Some of his reasons for rejecting the prevailing doctrines are as follows. First of all, he finds that the prevailing view involves various infinite regresses which the defenders of the prevailing view are unsuccessful in eliminating. In the second place, if a relation were something distinct from absolute things, God could produce it without also producing the terms. Hence God could produce paternity without any generation. Moreover, God could create two white things without anything else. But as it is

128. With the exception of the unilateral relations, e.g., as between creature and God, where the relational accident is only in one of the terms.

129. *Wilhelm von Ockham: Untersuchungen zur Ontologie der Ordnungen*, p. 146.

130. *Quodlibeta Septem*, vii, q. 8; cf. *Quaestio de Relatione* attributed to Ockham (*Franciscan Studies*, Vol. XI, nos. 3–4 [Sept.–Dec., 1951], p. 296).

unthinkable that these two white things were not similar, Ockham concludes that similarity is not such another thing as the adherents of the prevailing view suppose.

Many other arguments are adduced to refute the common doctrine that relations are accidents, which I shall pass over for brevity. But it is important to mention that the principle of parsimony is invoked by Ockham: whatever can be explained by supposing that relations are things distinct from absolute substances and qualities can more easily and simply be explained without this supposition.

Ockham's diagnosis of the postulation of the superfluous relational accidents is worth mentioning. The erroneous opinion has, Ockham thinks, two sources. One is defective translation of ancient discussion. The more important source, however, is the inveterate tendency of men to multiply entities according to the number of terms of discourse. The misunderstanding of the abstract terms of human discourse leads people to suppose that every such term expresses an externally existing essence. But the fact is that some terms have only a nominal definition to which no essence corresponds.

Ockham admits, of course, that there is order and unity in the universe, that there is objective similarity, causal connection, and the like. But he insists that this unity, similarity, causality, etc., consists only of the terms themselves and is conceived by relational concepts in the mind. These views are plausible in terms of his nominalistic explanation of the universal terms of discourse. For Ockham had established, at least to his own satisfaction, that all the realistic views about universal natures were logically incoherent, and therefore that resemblance or similarity can and must be explained exclusively in terms of the resembling individuals themselves. This being apparently the case, it seemed plausible to account for *similarity* in such a way that it can be reduced without remainder to the individual substances (or qualities) which are similar to one another.

Causal relations also seemed to him to be reducible to the agent and the patient and the internal changes in both, a view which the Aristotelian analysis of causation makes superficially plausible. It is true that Ockham maintained that a condition of causal transaction is the *approximation* of agent to patient. But even here, approximation is only the absence of a medium between two things, and, if the medium is considered to be a substantival reality (as it was), it was plausible to account for approximation solely in terms of the absence of an intervening medium rather than a positive reality of any kind.

The views of Gregory of Rimini not only confirm other views which we have found in earlier writers, but also have some interesting features of their own. In Distinction 28, Questions 1–3, of the First Book of his *Commentary on the Sentences*, Gregory discusses the questions concerning the reality and distinction of relations. The first question is whether a relation is an existing thing independent of any operation of the mind. Although he will affirm this question, his arguments in the negative exclude one possibility at the outset, namely, the view that a relation is some connection intermediate between two extremes, for he holds that no such entity can exist in nature. This point is emphasized later on in the body of Question 2.

In order to answer the question whether relations really exist independently of any operation of the mind, he begins by distinguishing three senses of the word *relation*. As a single term, in contradistinction to a statement, the word *relation* is the same as the *relative*, i.e., the word *relation* stands for a thing which is said to be in relation. The word *relation*, however, can also mean that by which a relative is relative. There are two cases of this. The first is what Gregory calls that which is signifiable in a complex way, that is to say, the referent of a statement or propositional thought. Thus, the relation of a father to a son obtains because the one generates the other. Another sense of relation is that which is signifiable in a non-propositional way. In this sense *relation* is something which is the referent of an abstract term, as when we say that *similarity* is that by means of which something is similar to something, or when we say that *knowledge* is that by means of which a knower knows.

He then sets forth the following three conclusions: First, in the first sense of the term *relation*, a relation is a real thing existing outside the mind independent of any operation of the mind. The second conclusion is that no relation, in the second sense of the term, is a thing or entity existing outside of the mind. He expressly tells us that he takes the words *thing* and *entity* to be synonymous for the purpose of the present discussion.[131] The third conclusion is that a relation in the third sense of the term is something actually existing outside the soul and independent of its operation. Gregory proves the first conclusion by a number of arguments of which the following seem the most important. If no relation existed outside the soul and independent of the soul's activity, nothing could properly be denoted by a relative term. But the consequent is false, for if it were true, there would not even be two things actually distinct from one another prior to any activity of consciousness and all would be one, which is false. Moreover, no two things would be similar or equal. It is interesting to note that these arguments are directed against Petrus Aureoli and William of Ockham. Aureoli had argued that a relation exists "potentially" outside the mind, and is actual only as the work of the mind.[132] Ockham had argued that relations are terms either of discourse or of thought.

The second conclusion, that no relation exists outside the mind taken as signifiable by a proposition, is proved in three ways. In the first place, every entity falls under one of the categories. Nothing signifiable in a propositional way (*significabile complexe*) is a substance, a quantity, a quality, or anything falling under any other category. It follows that nothing signifiable in a

131. Gregory of Rimini, *Sententiarum*, i, d. 28, q. 1, a. 1. Contrast and compare *ibid.*, d. 1, q. 1, a. 1, Q.

132. See J. Paulus, *Henri de Gand* (Paris, 1938), p. 192, no. 2; B. Lindner, "Die Erkenntnislehre des Thomas von Strassburg," *Beiträge zur Geschichte der Philosophie des Mittelalters*, XXVII (1930), 113–20.

propositional way is an entity. Everyone would agree to the major premiss of this argument. The minor can be established as follows: None of the things falling under any of the categories is a complex (where a "complex" means an affirmation or a negation).[133] A second argument shows that if we admitted that the signification of propositions were entities, it would follow that there are necessary beings other than God. For there are truly necessary propositions about creatures, both affirmative hypothetical and categorical negative propositions. But nothing absolutely necessary exists independent of God. The final argument (which alone would suffice) is this: It is obvious to everyone that it would be quite unintelligible to maintain that "Socrates generates Plato" is an entity. For if we take the words "Socrates generates Plato" as suppositing personally and significatively (i.e., if we *use* this sentence rather than *mention* it), it is clear that we have no entity here. For all these reasons, then, a relation, in the second sense, is not an entity.

We turn to the third conclusion. That by means of which one thing is formally like another thing is a relation. Now there is something external to the soul and existing independently of the soul's activity by means of which one thing is formally like another thing. Hence there is something which is similitude or relation. The major premiss is plainly true, and the minor is established by the fact that it is by means of quality that one thing is like another outside the soul and independent of any mental activity. For example, it is by means of whiteness that one thing is white just as another thing is white. However, although in some cases the abstract term of relation refers to something outside the soul distinct from substances but inhering in them (*whiteness, science, love,* by which things are similar or knowers or lovers), this is not universally the case. In the instances of *same, different, contrary, creator* and *created,* the abstract terms do not stand for things inhering in substances. Thus when it is said that Socrates

133. Cf. Aristotle, *Categories,* chap. 4, 1ᵇ 25–27; *Metaphysics,* E, 4, 1027ᵇ 29–30.

is distinct from Plato, we do not denote any entity (such as "distinctness") which inheres in Socrates. We simply mean that Socrates is a being and Plato is a being and Socrates is not Plato. In fact, if every relative were relative by something formally inhering in it, it would follow that there are actually infinitely many things. For the inhering quality would require another inhering quality by which it inheres, and so on ad infinitum. Finally, when a person is said to be a father by means of "paternity," this abstract term must be taken to refer to the proposition signifying that the person in question has generated a son. And it has already been shown that the significatum of a proposition is not an entity.

This view of the matter naturally suggests to Gregory the question whether a relation is an entity wholly distinct from every absolute thing. Many people have held such a view, and have reasoned as follows: just as an individual is qualitatively such or such by an inhering quality, so an individual is relative by a relational accident formally inhering in it. But such an opinion is neither rational nor true.

Accordingly, Gregory sets forth the following conclusions about this question: (1) every entity is absolute; (2) every entity is relative; (3) not every entity is formally relative by an entity formally inhering in the relative; (4) something *is* relative by means of a formally inhering entity; (5) no relative is formally relative by means of some entity inhering in it which is distinct from every absolute entity whatever. It follows from this that no relation is an entity distinct from all absolute entities. What this all means is somewhat elucidated by Gregory's definition of *absolute* and *relative* things. An absolute thing is one which is said to be something "to itself," i.e., it is not said with inference *to another*. E.g., *man, stone, whiteness, sweetness* are absolute terms. Relative terms, on the other hand, are always said to be something *to another thing*, e.g., *father, son; double, half;* and the like.

I shall not go into the proof of these contentions but shall simply indicate that Gregory deduces the fifth conclusion and its corollary from the first conclusion. It is clear that Gregory rejects all attempts to introduce special relational accidents whose whole nature consists in being *to something.*

If we were to attempt to trace the doctrine just set forth, we would say that it has some of its roots in the opinion attributed to Averroes,[134] that the same objects belong to different categories so that an object can be both a substance and a relation.

Gregory of Rimini is thus opposed to special relational accidents as well as to any tie that extends from the referent to the relatum of a relation; indeed, he repeatedly states that the latter conception must be utterly rejected. In his reply to Scotus' arguments he is especially emphatic on both these points.[135]

9 · *Modern Views*

The medieval views about the nature of relations appear to determine the views of the seventeenth-century philosophers. Descartes, for example, treats *order* and *number* as being merely the modes under which we consider the things which are ordered and numbered.[136] His argument against the vacuum [137] shows that he cannot conceive of a distance as a relation. Spinoza is more explicit on the subject. In the *Metaphysical Thoughts* (Part I, chap. 5) *order* and *relation* are included in the list of notions which are only modes of thought by which we more easily re-member or imagine objects, and in the *Short Treatise* (Part I, chap. 10), relations are called *entia rationis* and said to be "our

134. See Krempel, *La Doctrine de la relation chez St. Thomas,* pp. 492–93, and Horten, *Die Metaphysik des Averroes.* Krempel's wording may be translated as: "Fire *qua* fire, belongs to the category of substance; but fire *qua* cause belongs to the category of relation" (p. 493). See above, p. 95.

135. *Sententiarum,* i, d. 28, q. 2, fol. 137 G.

136. *Principles of Philosophy,* Part I, Principle 55. Cf. *ibid.,* Part II, Prin-ciples 8 and 14.

137. *Ibid.,* Part II, Principle 18.

own creation," "not in nature," etc. That relations are the work of the mind is also held by Gassendi.[138] Hobbes intimates that relations are, as far as their extra-cognitive status goes, the same as the accidents which found the relations, the relation itself being a comparison which we make.[139]

Locke's position contains some ambiguities. On the one hand, he calls *relation* one class of complex ideas which consists in the consideration and comparing one *idea* with another.[140] Again, relations are "extraneous and superinduced" upon substances as being the product of the mind's composing activity. On the other hand, there is a basis for such comparison in things themselves.[141] Berkeley's remarks on the subject are not as clear as they might have been. We have, we are told, a notion of relation between things or ideas which is distinct from the things or ideas related because we can perceive the latter without the former.[142] Further, because relations include an act of the mind, we are more properly said to have a *notion* than an idea of the relations and habitudes of things. This *suggests* that relations are mental activities. But in many passages Berkeley tells us that "we perceive a continual succession of ideas," that we perceive "certain ideas of sense constantly *followed* [my italics] by other ideas," and he writes of "the experience we have had of the train and succession of ideas." [143]

138. *Syntagmata Philosophiae Epicurei*, II, sec. 1, 15.

139. *Elements of Philosophy*, Part II, chap. 11, sec. 6 (*English Works*, ed. W. Molesworth [London, 1839–1845], I, 135).

140. *Essay concerning Human Understanding*, Book II, chap. 11, par. 4 and par. 7 (see *John Locke: An Essay concerning Human Understanding*, ed. A. C. Fraser [Oxford, 1894], I, 204–5).

141. *Ibid.*, chap. 25, par. 8 (ed. Fraser, I, 430). See also R. I. Aaron, *John Locke* (Oxford, 1937), pp. 174–89.

142. *Principles of Human Knowledge*, secs. 89, 142. See A. A. Luce and T. E. Jessop, eds., *Works of George Berkeley*, II (London, 1948), 106, note 1: "Berkeley nowhere develops this view of relations, which seems to imply that relations among 'ideas' are not discovered but instituted by the mental act, or at any rate that the activity of relating somehow enters into the content of the relation."

143. *Principles of Human Knowledge*, secs. 26, 32, 59 (Luce and Jessop, eds., *Works of George Berkeley*, II, 52, 54, 66). Cf. secs. 95, 112, 145.

That Berkeley was not clear on the matter, therefore, seems evident.

The most extensive discussion of relations in early modern philosophy is to be found in the writings of Leibniz, where the influence of the medieval tradition is most obvious. Leibniz had special reasons for adopting medieval views on the subject. If there were real connections among things, the doctrine that the predicate of every true affirmative proposition is contained in the subject could not be maintained, and this doctrine is surely central to Leibniz's thought.

Relations and orders are 'beings of reason' although they have their foundation in things, namely, in the Supreme Reason. Several arguments are given for this. Leibniz repeatedly uses the argument that an accident cannot be in two subjects.[144] Again, Leibniz argues that "where there are only entities by aggregation, there will be no real entities. What is not truly *one* entity, is not truly an *entity*." [145] This is the old maxim to the effect that *Ens et unum convertuntur*, and Leibniz does not hesitate to place this at the beginning of the *Monadology* and the *Principles of Nature and Grace*.

Leibniz does not deny that there are intramonadic relations. In fact, his conception of the individual monad as determined by its initial state which contains the law of the series of states through which it will pass necessarily involves some kind of relation. Thus, though relations between monads can only be *phenomena bene fundata*, the intramonadic succession of states can by no means be phenomenal merely.

Hume's doctrine of relations is complicated by several features of his philosophy. That relations are not properties of things but

144. *Die Philosophischen Schriften von G. W. Leibniz,* ed. Gerhardt, II, 486 and 457. Also, Leibniz's *5th Paper to Clarke,* sec. 42; *New Essays,* Book II, chap. 12, sec. 7. As I have indicated earlier, this argument occurs in Avicenna, Aquinas, Albertus Magnus, and Suarez (*Disputationes Metaphysicae,* Disputatio XLVII, sec. 6, no. 4).

145. Letter to Arnauld, 30 April 1687. See *Lettres de Leibniz à Arnauld,* ed. Geneviève Lewis (Paris, 1952), p. 69.

rather arise "from the comparison which the mind makes"[146] is explicitly stated. The philosophical relations of resemblance, degrees of quantity, degrees of quality, are described as "that particular circumstance, in which, even upon the arbitrary union of two ideas in the fancy, we may think proper to compare them."[147] We are further informed that these are "such as depend entirely on the ideas, which we compare together."[148] Finally, the long footnote to the section "Of Abstract Ideas"[149] states that the point or circumstance of resemblance is neither distinct nor separable from that in which two different simple ideas resemble one another. All this suggests that such relations are not distinct from the items which are, by comparison, discovered to be resembling.

The other class of relations, which includes those of space and time, are said to be able to be changed, without any change in the ideas,[150] and this suggests that such relations are distinct from their terms. These are also described as the "manner" in which impressions occur together or in succession,[151] and this "manner" is sometimes discussed in such a way as to lead the reader to believe that it is distinguishable (and, therefore, on Hume's terms, separable) from the several impressions thus or thus deployed. Yet such a view would seem to be incompatible with what Hume holds elsewhere. For it is one of the principles of his philosophy that complex impressions are reducible without remainder to their simple constituents.

This is re-enforced by Hume's doctrine that the only true units are those incapable of further reduction.[152] This view is, ultimately, derived from a rigorous application of the principle that

146. *Treatise of Human Nature*, Book I, Part 2, sec. 4 (Everyman's Library edition [London, 1911], I, 52).
147. *Ibid.*, Part 1, sec. 5 (Everyman ed., I, 22).
148. *Ibid.*, Part 3, sec. 1 (Everyman ed., I, 73).
149. *Ibid.*, Part 1, sec. 7 (Everyman ed., I, 28).
150. *Ibid.*, Part 3, sec. 1 (Everyman ed., I, 73).
151. *Ibid.*, Part 2, sec. 3.
152. *Ibid.*, sec. 2.

the essential unities are the basic existences on which everything else depends. Thus, while Hume allows that there are successions and juxtapositions of impressions and in some places goes so far as to say that these are *not* created by mental activities,[153] it is almost or entirely impossible to make them consistent with the doctrine that complex impressions are wholly reducible to their simple constituents.

The explicit view that relations are entirely the work of the mind has been attributed to Kant with considerable justification. Kant maintained that "That in which alone the sensations can be posited and ordered [*sich ordnen*] in a certain form, cannot itself be sensation, . . ." [154] and that the sensations themselves have no extensive but only intensive magnitude.[155] It is the forms of intuition which give relations spatial and temporal to the un-ordered manifold of sensation; in fact, these forms of intuition contain nothing but relations.[156] It is by a property of our mind, the form of outer sense, that we represent the shape, magnitude, and relation of things to one another.[157]

That relations are contributed by the mind to the congeries of sensations is, in fact, one of the main contentions of Kant against empiricism as he understood it. And, as Hobhouse observed, an answer to Kant involves a re-assessment of the "given" element in knowledge.[158]

There is much that could and should be said about the concept of relation, both in the development of absolute idealism and in the further development of empiricism in the nineteenth century. This would involve another investigation at least as extensive in

153. *Ibid.*, Part 3, sec. 14.
154. *Kritik der reinen Vernunft, Transcendental Aesthetik,* A 20 (trans. N. K. Smith, *Immanuel Kant's Critique of Pure Reason* [London, 1950], p. 66).
155. *Ibid.*, B 207.
156. *Ibid.*, B 67.
157. *Ibid.*, B 37.
158. L. T. Hobhouse, *The Theory of Knowledge* (London, 1896), pp. 38 ff.

scope as the present one. But there is little likelihood that anything like a satisfactory view has come from these philosophical endeavors.

The contemporary view of relations is due mainly to the development of the logic of relations by Charles Peirce, Schroeder, and more especially by Frege and Russell. We owe to Russell, more than to any other single philosopher, a clear understanding of the nature and importance of relations. His critique of previous views was, in my opinion, decisive, and he made it abundantly clear that a radical innovation in metaphysics is involved in his view that dyadic relations are not reducible to monadic attributes of their terms.

The doctrine of substance and accident in its historical form determined an erroneous view of relations. The influence of the substance-accident ontology persisted after the doctrine itself had been radically modified or abandoned. This is due, in part at least, to the failure to see at once the full implications of criticism. But there were doubtless other causes, some of them psychological in nature.

It was perhaps difficult to see how relations are represented in discourse, especially when there is a tendency to say that individual expressions stand for individual things. How relational symbols function in discourse requires considerable elucidation, which is easier to manage in terms of the modern logical relations than in the times before these relations were invented. In an important sense, a primitive relation can only be exhibited by the form of relational expressions, and relational expressions do not stand for items in the extra-discursive world in the way individual expressions do.[159]

Another cause which probably tended to make relations recessive and terms of relations dominant is the following: The process of learning to use both proper and common nouns appears to require from nature and experience a certain steady constellation

159. B. Russell, *Outline of Philosophy* (London, 1927), 275.

of mutually cohering qualities. In semi-Kantian language, if there were no steady constellation of cohering qualities to which teacher and learner could refer again and again, it would be difficult or impossible to learn the referent of certain word-sounds and so difficult or impossible to learn the meaning of proper and common nouns. Thus the acquisition of language requires us to collect under one term of discourse those qualities which mutually cohere in our experience. But this is not all. We tend to include in the meaning of noun-substantives, not only the steady qualities but also the characteristic modes of behavior of such groups of cohering qualities vis-à-vis other such groups. Thus not only do names of artifacts, such as *knife* or *house*, bring to our mind the steady qualities by which we recognize the referents of these terms, but the characteristic and expected behavior of such things is also thought of. We include in the "meaning" of such terms their characteristic function or purpose. In other words, we "read" into the referent of names the modes of behavior we expect from those referents. Now all this has two main effects: first, it concentrates attention on the referents of nouns, and second, it tends to absorb the meaning of transitive verbs into that of their nominatives, accusatives, datives, etc. This, then, is surely one natural way in which relationships tend to become the recessive, and "things" related tend to become the dominant features of conscious experience.

Another probable source of the tendency to "absorb" relationships into their terms is due to unconscious analogies we tend to draw between ourselves and the world. Our affective states (loving, fearing, etc.) we think of as *in* ourselves even though their objects are, we suppose, external to ourselves. It is easy to allow the affective state to supplant the relation between ourselves and the putative object of these states. Doubtless, much could be said on this aspect of the subject.

My concern here, however, has been with the influence of explicit theories, rather than natural or acquired propensities of human beings in their philosophically innocent states. The main influences I have attempted to sketch have been (1) the doctrine that *being* and *unity* are convertible terms, and (2) the doctrine that relations are accidents. In the historical contexts of these two doctrines, the concept of a relation as a feature of facts which involves two terms taken together was impossible. The best minds of the medieval traditions saw the peculiarities involved in relational facts, and occasionally were on the verge of a correct solution. Thus both St. Thomas and St. Albert realized the two-fold dependence of relations, and William of Ockham saw that relational terms can only be predicated *conjunctively*. But the need for unilateral relations prevented the medievals from achieving a correct understanding.

Historical Remarks
on Some Medieval Views
of Induction

Francis Bacon must be accorded the honor of having presented the first *systematic* account of induction by elimination, and his claims to originality, although exaggerated, have a real basis. His criticism of his predecessors was severe, and it is worthwhile to attempt to discover to what extent it was justified. It will be impossible to answer this question with any completeness until many more late medieval texts are available to us in critical editions. In the present state of our knowledge we can nevertheless show that the medieval philosophers were concerned with the nature of inductive reasoning, and we can discover to what extent they were moving toward modern views on this subject. It will be found that some of the representative thinkers of antiquity and the Middle Ages developed a theory of induction, mainly from suggestions in the writings of Aristotle, which, although in some ways it anticipates modern views, moves mainly along quite different lines.

1 · Ancient Views

Although induction of general principles from the painstaking observation of particulars is especially clear in the case of some of the earlier parts of the Hippocratic corpus, we must turn to the writings of Plato to see the first hint or suggestion which is later developed by Aristotle into an explicit theory of induction.

Although his low estimate of physical reality relegates the sensible world to a lower order than the world of the Forms, Plato unquestionably thought that experience of the physical world contributed in some way to the acquisition of genuine knowledge. Thus we read in the *Phaedrus* that "man must needs understand the language of forms, passing from a plurality of perceptions to a unity gathered together by reasoning; and such understanding is a recollection of those things which our souls beheld aforetimes . . . ." [1] In the later dialogues there is an increasing emphasis on the importance of sensory cognition. In the *Timaeus* we find an apostrophe to the sense of sight to which our knowledge of number and the nature of the universe is ascribed. [2] Even philosophy owes its origin to the sense of sight. And similar praises are bestowed on the sense of hearing. But this suggestion must not be misunderstood. Plato's doctrine of recollection is never explicitly abandoned, and all these praises of our senses must be understood in the context of that doctrine. Our senses stimulate the recollection of the Forms in one way and dialectic does this in another.

1. *Phaedrus*, 249 B–C (trans. R. Hackforth, *Plato's Phaedrus* [New York, 1952], p. 86).
2. *Timaeus*, 47 A–B.

Still the true reality is cognized by thought alone, however much sensory stimulation and dialectic may serve to trigger the recollection of Forms. Something like the process which Aristotle later describes as induction is suggested in these passages. It is also worth observing, as Bacon himself noticed, that the method of induction resembles the elenctic dialogue. But as we shall see, the inductions described by Aristotle and those which Bacon recommended are, in important ways, quite different.

When Aristotle abandoned the doctrine of separate forms and Plato's doctrine of reminiscence, it was inevitable that induction assume an important rôle in the acquisition of knowledge. For Aristotle the highest form of knowing concerns the universal concepts and universal propositions. At the same time the only realities outside consciousness are individuals, and, in the first instance, individuals accessible to perception. The universal concepts and propositions being concerned with individuals, it is necessary that we begin with perception and somehow derive universal concepts and propositions from this source. Aristotle thus is convinced that sense-perception is indispensable to knowledge:[3] a loss or absence of any of the senses involves a loss or absence of the corresponding knowledge, for universals can only be grasped by induction from particulars and only by perception do we grasp the particulars. Moveover, Aristotle assumes that the world is essentially knowable. Not only does he hold that the soul is in a sense all existing things,[4] but he also holds that we have sense-organs capable of detecting whatever is perceptible.[5] This view of the matter is of considerable significance for Aristotle and those who followed him in the account of induction.

We must now turn attention to some of Aristotle's assumptions about the nature of things. Aristotle supposed that all individuals of a kind, specific or generic, possessed similar causal characteristics. For the second actuality, which consists of the operation

3. *Posterior Analytics*, i, 18, 81ª 38.
4. *De Anima*, iii, 8, 431ᵇ 21.
5. *Ibid.*, 1, 424ᵇ 20–425ª 15.

(i.e., the actual behavior of a thing), depends on the first actuality, which is the form, or, in the case of organic beings, the soul. The potentialities, active or passive, possessed by things of a given kind depend on the actualities. Moreover, the same causal characteristic or potentiality cannot, in numerically different instances, depend on radically distinct actualities. For actuality is prior to potentiality and therefore the character of potential or actual effects depends necessarily on that of the cause.

Aristotle regularly assumes that whatever passes from a state of potentiality to a state of actuality does so only by virtue of an actual agent.[6] This may be called a form of the Principle of Causality. He also assumes that the same cause in the same condition always produces the same effect,[7] and he views this principle as closely connected with the notion of final cause.[8] The only exception to this rule is the case of rational potencies which are disposed to contrary effects.[9] (This exception is of some importance to the medievals, particularly to Duns Scotus' account of induction.[10]) This may be called the Principle of Causation. Finally, as I have already noted, Aristotle denies the real plurality of causes [11] on the ground that an effect must be like its cause. This principle may be called the Resemblance of Effects and Causes. (The problem of univocal and equivocal causes may be neglected here for a time, although it assumes some importance later on.) All these principles must be kept in mind when we attempt to discover how Aristotle understands induction.

We now turn to *induction* itself as Aristotle uses the term. I

6. *Metaphysics*, Λ, 6, 1071ᵇ 29–31; *Physics*, viii, 5, 257ᵇ 9; also, *Metaphysics*, K, 8, 1049ᵇ 23; *Physics*, vii, 1, 241ᵇ 25, and viii, 1, 251ᵃ 10.

7. *De Generatione et Corruptione*, ii, 10, 336ᵃ 27–28.

8. *Physics*, viii, 1, 252ᵃ 11–12; *De Caelo*, iii, 2, 301ᵃ 5; *De Generatione Animalium*, iii, 10, 760ᵃ 31.

9. *Metaphysics*, Θ, 5, 1048ᵃ 8; *Physics*, viii, 1, 251ᵃ 28 ff; *De Interpretatione*, chap. 13, 22ᵇ 38—23ᵃ 3.

10. *Opus Oxoniense*, i, d. 3, q. 4 (trans. Allan B. Wolter, O.F.M., *Duns Scotus: Philosophical Writings* [Edinburgh, 1962], pp. 109–11.

11. See especially *Posterior Analytics*, ii, 16–18.

discern a number of uses of epagoge which have in common the passage from cases to a universal proposition.[12] Sometimes, this is a passage from *all* cases of a generalization to the generalization itself,[13] but "more often only some of the" cases.[14]

It is better to divide the uses of epagoge in another way. (1) The account of induction which Aristotle gives in *Metaphysics*, A, 1, 981ª, *Posterior Analytics*, ii, 19, 99ᵇ 35—100ᵇ 17, and *Rhetoric*, i, 2, 1356ᵇ 25–32 is concerned with the passage from individuals to the generalization about all individuals of a given kind. (2) The induction discussed in *Prior Analytics*, ii, 23, 68ᵇ 15–30 is plainly a passage from *all* (or presumably all) the species of a genus to a generalization about the genus. Many applications of this sort of induction are to be found throughout Aristotle's writings.[15] (3) Finally, I believe that there is another form of generalization which is arrived at by an inductive process. This is the process by which we "grasp the analogy" in comprehending the terms of metaphysics, especially potency and act.[16] I believe that this process is distinguishable from the two aforementioned, and that, probably, Aristotle supposed that such an induction provided us, not only with the "concepts" of metaphysics, but also with the basic metaphysical truths, and in particular, those which state the various maxims of causality, causation, etc.

It is clear that the first two kinds of induction are of most importance if we are interested in establishing the basic propositions of some particular science or in apprehending the specific or generic universals. The grasp of a specific universal is described

12. See also W. D. Ross, *Aristotle's Prior and Posterior Analytics: A Revised Text with Introduction and Commentary* (Oxford, 1949), p. 47 ff.

13. *Prior Analytics*, ii, 23, 68ᵇ 20–21; *Metaphysics*, I, 4, 1055ᵇ 5–10.

14. Ross, *Commentary on Analytics*, p. 48. Cf. *Topics*, i, 2, 105ª 13–16, and ii, 7, 113ᵇ 15—114ª 6; *Physics*, iv, 3, 210ª 15—210ᵇ 9; *De Partibus Animalium*, ii, 1, 646ª 24–30; *Metaphysics*, Δ, 29, 1025ª 6–13, and Θ, 6, 1048ª 35—1048ᵇ 4.

15. E.g., *Physics*, iv, 2, 210ᵇ 8–10, and v, 1, 224ᵇ 28–30; *Metaphysics*, I, 3, 1054ᵇ 33, and 4, 1055ᵇ 17.

16. *Metaphysics*, Θ, 6, 1048ª 30—1048ᵇ 9.

explicitly in *Metaphysics* [17] and *Posterior Analytics*,[18] and it may seem, at first sight, that there is an important difference between these two accounts, because the one in *Metaphysics* is concerned with universal propositions, whereas the discussion in *Posterior Analytics* is concerned with universal concepts. I think this difference is relatively unimportant. For, if we consider that a concept is a sort of telescoped proposition, the difference is of minor importance.

This account of induction from individuals to a universal proposition or to a universal concept is obscure in a number of details. We are told that the repetition of sensations is mnemonically retained and out of these several memories comes a single "experience" (ἐμπειρία). Ross, in a note, says that "experience . . . is a coagulation of memories . . . . (*a*) as embodying the data of unconsciously selected awarenesses it foreshadows a universal; but (*b*) as not conscious of what in the past is relevant, and why, it is not aware of it as universal." [19] There is some evidence for this in *De Anima*, iii, 11, 434ᵃ 7 ff, where Aristotle says that it is possible to *make* one (ἕν) out of many images (φαντάσματα); in *De Anima*, iii, 4, 430ᵃ, where the potential intellect is compared to a tablet which is empty but potentially written upon; and in *De Memoria*, chapter 1, 450ᵇ, where we find the comparison with the imprint of a seal. And John Philoponus supports this when he states that the process involves a superimposition of images so that the common features of the several images are thus re-enforced.[20] The process thus seems to be a sort of automatic occurrence of the Figure of Agreement (in Mill's sense). Yet there is surely more to the matter than just this, because the final "intuition" (νοῦς) certainly adds something, and it is here, I think, that we

17. In Book A, chapter 1.
18. In Book ii, chapter 19.
19. W. D. Ross, *Aristotle's Metaphysics: A Revised Text with Introduction and Commentary* (Oxford, 1924), I, 116–17.
20. *In Aristotelis Analytica Posteriora Commentarium*, ed. M. Wallies (Berlin, 1909), p. 437 l. 26.

must find the difference between mere *experience* and *science* or *art*. But what is it that emerges from this process? Sometimes Aristotle speaks as if the intuition involves the direct grasp of a universal concept or proposition so that we *see* the necessity that things of a certain kind possess such or such potentialities (properties). At other times, he seems far more cautious and suggests that induction can only reveal the *fact* that things of a kind have a certain specifiable potentiality, and that our knowledge of what the causal characteristics of things are is only a step in the direction of seeing *why* things of such a kind possess such characteristics.

In fact, it is plausible to assume that the general causal maxims, i.e., causality, causation, and the mutual resemblance of causes and effects (as defined above), are principles which make Aristotelian induction possible. If we possess certain organs and faculties and if the physical world is essentially perceptible, the regularities will be eventually observed, and the general maxims together with experience will enable man to obtain universal knowledge.

The universal regularities in Aristotle's sub-lunar world are not invariable but only "for the most part." But what occurs "for the most part" in a determinate order cannot be due to chance. In the works of nature only impediments or incomplete development prevent invariable repetitions and sequences.[21]

Induction of the first kind then, i.e., from individuals to a concept or universal proposition, arises from the sensations of a finite number of individuals (thus never from *all* the individuals, because they are potentially infinite in number), and is supported by the general propositions about causality, causation, resemblance of causes and effects, and the denial of chance as an explanation of very frequent repetition.

In the only place where Aristotle discusses induction of the second kind,[22] he explicitly requires that it take account of *all* the cases. The cases here are, as is plain from the illustration, *all*

21. *Physics*, ii, 8, 199ᵇ 15–20.
22. *Prior Analytics*, ii, 23.

the species of a genus. In fact, the inductive syllogism would be invalid if this were not so.

As far as I can tell, the third kind of induction, viz., the inductive process which enables us to grasp the analogies that provide us with the very general concepts and propositions of metaphysics regarding the principles of causality and so forth, requires a radically different account. For, if it is correct that the inductions of the first two kinds require completion by way of very general assumptions about the natural world, metaphysical induction itself, which provides these very general assumptions, must be completed in a different way. There is, in fact, a fundamental difficulty about establishing the principles of metaphysics which was noticed both by Avicenna [23] and by Aquinas.[24] There are indications that Aristotle thought that the basic principles of first philosophy, although they are derived from experience like all other basic propositions, are finally grasped by intuition as self-evident.[25]

It is worth noting that Aristotle discusses other subsidiary forms of inductive reasoning, such as *example* (i.e., reasoning by analogy *or* reasoning from particulars to other particulars),[26] and the argument from signs [27] which are discussed by several of the medievals both in Islam and in Christendom. It is also worth noting that the Principle of Parsimony is stated by Aristotle in several places.[28]

I should mention some post-Aristotelian developments of the subject of induction before going on to the medievals. The Stoics conceded grudgingly a minor rôle to induction in order to ac-

23. *Metaphysica,* tract i, chap. 3.

24. *In Boethium de Trinitate,* q. 5, a. 1, reply to 9th objection.

25. E.g., *Physics,* viii, 1, 251[a] 10, where he states that even apart from the definition of motion (which assures us that each kind of motion necessarily involves the presence of the things that are capable of that kind of motion in virtue of the meaning or definition of *motion)* it is generally admitted that it is what is capable of motion that is in motion. There are a number of such appeals to definition to establish a general principle.

26. *Prior Analytics,* ii, 24, 68[b] 38; *Rhetoric,* i, 2, 1357[b] 25–35.

27. *Prior Analytics,* ii, 27, 70[a] 6 ff.

28. *Physics,* i, 7, 190[a] 1–7 and viii, 6, 259[a] 12; *De Caelo,* i, 4, 271[a] 34, and iii, 4, 302[b] 21; *Metaphysics,* Δ, 6, 1016[a] 12 ff.

count for divination,[29] but their major concern appears to have been with the development of the logic of propositions, the purpose of which was to infer the unknown from the known.[30] The Epicureans, on the other hand, placed considerable emphasis on induction. Epicurus emphasized the need to confirm the initial deliverances of sensation by subsequent induction,[31] and the method of pluralistic explanation of phenomena has an inductive feature.[32] Perhaps the most interesting aspect of the Epicurean trust in induction is that the proof of *Ex nihilo nihil fit* is, unlike earlier attempts, a clearly inductive argument.[33] The remains of Philodemus [34] reveal a detailed critique of Stoic inference and a defence of the argument from analogy.[35]

Finally, the Sceptical critique of induction is worth mentioning for two reasons: (1) It seems likely that it was directed against Aristotelian induction, because, according to Sextus Empiricus,[36] we cannot be sure that we have taken account of (*a*) all individuals of a species, or (*b*) all species of a genus. (2) There is no evidence that the Greek Sceptics directed their attention to the difficulties about induction which are principally associated with the name of Hume.[37]

29. See E. Bréhier, *Chrysippe et l'ancien stoïcisme* (Paris, 1951), p. 75, and V. C. L. Brochard, "La Logique des Stoïciens," *Études de philosophie anciénne et de philosophie moderne* (Paris, 1926), p. 224.

30. Diogenes Laertius, vii, 45, 52, 62; Sextus Empiricus, *Adversus Mathematicos*, vii, 25.

31. See Letter to Herodotus, Diogenes Laertius, x, 50, *et passim;* Lucretius, *De Rerum Natura*, iv, 454.

32. See Letter to Pythocles, Diogenes Laertius, x, 94, 99, 100, *et passim*.

33. See Letter to Herodotus, Diogenes Laertius, x, 39; Lucretius, *De Rerum Natura*, i, 125 ff.

34. P. H. De Lacey and E. A. De Lacey, *Philodemus: On Methods of Inference* (Philadelphia, 1941), sec. XVI, ll. 16–23.

35. *Ibid.*, sec. VIII, l. 32–sec. IX, l. 3.

36. *Pyrrhonic Hypotyposes*, ii, 195–97.

37. E. Zeller, *Die Philosophie der Griechen, Teil III, Abteilung 2: Die Nacharistotelische Philosophie*, 2te Hälfte (Leipzig, 1868), pp. 38–39; F. Überweg, *Grundriss der Geschichte der Philosophie*, trans. G. S. Morris, *A History of Philosophy from Thales to the Present Time* (New York,

The few remarks of Aristotle on the induction from individuals to the species are quite obscure, as Bonitz observed.[38] It is plausible to suppose that his two discussions of this sort of induction occur within a framework of assumptions which he takes for granted in any such discussion, e.g., the assumption that a change of a given kind must always be brought about by an appropriate and actual mover. (Such an assumption, as I have just formulated it, is a conflation of many statements found throughout his writings and puts together his doctrines of potentiality and actuality, of the priority of the actual, his teleology, etc.) But it also quite possible that Aristotle does not presuppose all these views on physical and metaphysical matters. Until we have more assurance about the order of composition of Aristotle's writings, we must not speculate further. As matters stand, Aristotle's accounts of induction do not *explicitly* assume the views developed in the *Physics* and *Metaphysics*.

The medieval writers who took Aristotle (mainly) as their point of departure had no questions of this sort in mind. But they must have been puzzled by the extraordinary brevity and conciseness of Aristotle's remarks about an admittedly fundamental subject. The primary premisses of any science cannot be demonstrated. The primary concepts cannot be obtained by an explicitly necessary process. Yet all we are explicitly told is that induction (together with the intuition which terminates induction) provides the primary concepts and principles.

It is possible to conjecture why Aristotle treated the induction of concepts and the induction of principles in very much the same way. There are, doubtless, resemblances between the psycholog-

---

1872), I, 217. The Greek commentaries on *Metaphysics* A and on *Posterior Analytics* ii (those of Themistius [A.D. 317–388], a paraphrase which was translated into Latin from Arabic; Philoponus [A.D. 490–530]; an anonymous commentary on the second book; Eustratius [A.D. 1050–1120]) are of some help in understanding Aristotle's intentions but, as far as I know, make no decisive advances in the doctrine. Galen is worth further study, although here also there is not much evidence of any advance in a theory of induction.
  38. Hermann Bonitz, *Aristotelis Metaphysica*, II (Bonn, 1849), 29 and 410.

ical processes which lead to the formation of a concept and those which lead to the acceptance of a principle. In both cases the universal (whether concept or principle) emerges from the inspection of individuals and mnemonic retention of many such inspections. There is, however, an important difference between obtaining some concepts and obtaining universal propositions. In the former, we, let us at least assume, detect a feature repeated over and over again amidst differences. In the latter, we detect concomitances or sequences occurring again and again. The sort of question which can be asked about these concomitances or sequences is whether some cases will suffice to inform us of what would always happen if there be no interfering factors. This sort of question does not apply to some concepts. If we are concerned with the sort of concept which is a conjunctively complex set of simpler concepts, we can ask whether, if some constituents of such a complex are given, the remainder will be given. But what we would regard as a conjunctively complex concept is, I believe, what Aristotle regarded as an accidental unity, and the sorts of concepts which he was mainly concerned with were not of that sort. They were, rather, essential unities.

Another reason why Aristotle treated universal concepts and certain universal propositions in very similar ways is this. The concepts which he is mainly concerned with are defined concepts. The definitions are often of the sort that includes in the meaning of a term the cause of the attribute in question. Thus he defines eclipse and thunder in this way, and we may assume that this was his regular way. The definitions of *man* or *animal*, if we consider them carefully, include causal characteristics; in the one example, the capacity to reason, in the other, sensitive and motile capacities. Considered in this light, concepts and propositions are not so very different.

This leads, however, to a number of difficulties with which students of scientific method are still plagued to the present day. In fact, some of the problems of induction can be made to disappear by including the characteristic behavior of things of a certain kind in the meaning of the term that is used to denote the kind in question.

It is possible that Aristotle sometimes supposed that we could directly witness the exercise of causal efficacy; indeed, some of the things he says on various subjects might easily suggest that he held such a view.[39] In other passages, however, an entirely different impression is gained.

For illustrations of an entirely different attitude, we can cite a considerable number of passages in which Aristotle states that the principles of a science are usually or always last in the order of knowing. Thus we are usually obliged to start with the empirical facts before we can learn of causes and reasons. The *De Anima* tells us that "in the order of investigation the question of what an agent does precedes the question, what enables it to do what it does." [40] Having observed the results of the characteristic activities of an organic agent, we can reason to the powers necessary and sufficient for such activities. As a particular example of such reasoning we could cite the arguments for the existence of a "common sense." [41] In such arguments, powers are plainly inferred from operations, and certainly are not directly discerned. In sum, there are many cases in which the existence and nature of powers are *inferred* from the observed facts rather than intuited.

39. Eg., *Physics*, ii, 1, 193ª 1–6, states that the existence of things with an inherent principle of movement is evident and neither admits of, nor requires, demonstration; *De Generatione et Corruptione*, i, 1, 314ᵇ 13 ff, and i, 10, 327ª 17, insist that alteration and quantitative change are facts of observation.

40. *De Anima*, ii, 4, 415ª 18. All translations from Aristotle are taken from the text in the Oxford University Press's *Works of Aristotle*, ed. J. A. Smith and W. D. Ross (Oxford and London, 1910–1952).

41. *Ibid.*, iii, 1, 425ᵇ 11–427ª 15.

2 · *Medieval Doctrines*

The various medieval authors who attempted to extract a theory of induction from these somewhat enigmatic discussions in Aristotle seem to have taken the line that causal connection can be inferred from the regularity with which events of certain kinds occurred. As far as I have been able to discover, the main discussion of induction in the thirteenth and fourteenth centuries depends on the views of Avicenna.

The views of Avicenna on induction are of importance to us mainly because they undoubtedly influenced one of the most widely used discussions of Aristotle's doctrine, viz., Grosseteste's *Commentary on the Posterior Analytics*. Avicenna's *Logic* was very incompletely translated into Latin, but the essentials of his theory of induction are contained in Al-Ghazali's *Logic* (the first part of *The Tendencies of the Philosophers*, which is based entirely on Avicenna).[42]

---

42. In the Arabic and Persian original works of Avicenna, however, the subject is discussed in several places:

1) *Danesh Nameh*, trans. M. Achena and H. Massé, *Le Livre de Science*, I (Paris, 1955), 66 ff.

2) *Kitāb al-'Išārāt*, trans. A.-M. Goichon, *Le Livre des Directives et Remarques* (Beyrouth and Paris, 1951), p. 191 ff.

3) *Kitāb al-Najāt*, the portion translated by S. Pines in "La Conception de la Conscience de Soi chez Avicenne et chez Abu'l-Barakāt Al-Baghdādī," *Archives d' Histoire Doctrinale et Littéraire du Moyen Age*, XXI (1954), 96 ff.

4) *Kitāb al-Najāt*, the portion translated by F. Rahman in *Avicenna's Psychology: An English translation of Kitāb Al-Najāt Book II, Chapter VI* (Oxford University Press, London, 1952), p. 55.

5) The writing known as *Fī mā taqarrara 'indahu fī ḥujaj al-muthbitīn li'l-māḍī mabda'an zamāniyyan* ("On the opinion which is crystallized in one in what concerns the arguments of those who assert that the past has a

Avicenna distinguishes between *complete* and *incomplete* induction, and illustrates the danger of incomplete induction with an example which is used frequently by other writers (e.g., Averroes): the example of supposing that because most animals masticate by moving the lower jaw, all animals do so. The exception which falsifies this is the crocodile, which moves the upper jaw.[43] He also states that it is arguments of this sort that are believed by dialecticians and by the Mutakallimun. But the most interesting discussion of an induction which leads from individuals to the universal is as follows:

We have an experience, i.e., we have noticed over and over again, that administration of scammony [44] is followed by the purging of bile. Then an imperceived syllogism is produced in the mind to the effect that this sequence of events is not a matter of chance, for it would not be possible for such to occur so frequently if it were a matter of chance. Hence we can conclude that scammony *by its nature* is purgative of bile.[45] It is this argument

---

temporal beginning"), trans. Pines, "La Conception de la Conscience de Soi," *AHDL*, XXI, 95 ff.

6) The *Logical Part* of the *Kitāb al-Shifāʾ*.

There are also many secondary accounts derived from Avicenna, viz., Al-Ghazali's *Maḳaṣid al-Falasifah* (i, 4); M. Comtino's *Commentary on Maimonides' "Millot ha-Higgayon"* (H. A. Wolfson, *The Philosophy of Spinoza* [Cambridge, Mass., 1934], II, 135); Abu'l-Barakāt al-Baghdādī's (d. 1164) *Logic of Kitāb al-muʿtabar* (trans. Pines, "La Conception de la Conscience de Soi," *AHDL*, XXI, 97–98).

43. This fact was known to Herodotus (see ii, 68) and Aristotle mentions it several times (e.g., *Historia Animalium*, chap. 2, 494[b] 23). It was also used by Sextus Empiricus as an argument against induction (*Pyrrhonic Hypotyposes*, ii, 195, and see the comment of S. van den Bergh in his translation of Averroes' *Tahafut al-Tahafut* [London, 1954], II, 197).

44. Cf. F. A. Flückiger and D. Hanbury, *Pharmaco-graphica* (London, 1879), pp. 439 ff, which may be paraphrased as follows: Botanical origin. Convolvulus Scammania L., a twining plant much resembling convolvulus arvensis but having a stout taproot. Found in Syria, Asia Minor, Greece, etc. Medical use. The dried milky juice was used as a medicine from ancient times. Theophrastus, Dioscorides, Pliny, Celsus, Rufus of Ephesus all mention it. Also mentioned in Cicero (*De div.*) and Galen.

45. See that portion of *Kitāb al-Najāt* translated by S. Pines in "La Conception de la Conscience de Soi," *AHDL*, XXI, 96. Cf. A.-M. Goichon,

which will be used by Grosseteste,[46] Albertus Magnus,[47] and Duns Scotus,[48] and it is, doubtless, one of the bases of Ockham's discussion. The main principle underlying induction, viz., that what occurs frequently cannot be due to chance, is, as I have already noted, from Aristotle.[49]

Although Al-Ghazali contributed nothing directly to the subject of induction he had important views on the related subject of causality and causation. His views on causal connection are certainly not original since they were widely held by the orthodox theologians in Islam from the time of Al-Ashari (tenth century), but his statement of the position is doubtless his own. According to Al-Ghazali, causal connection is not necessary in any sense. There is no logical connection between any antecedent and any subsequent event. There is no contradiction in asserting that the antecedent event occurs and that the subsequent event does not. This logical argument is supplemented by an empirical argument. In any allegedly causal routine, e.g., contact of a flame with cloth and the subsequent combustion of the cloth, the only thing observable is the sequence of events, and this provides no evidence that the contact with flame was the cause of the combustion.[50] These arguments against the necessity or alleged discernment of causal efficacy occur again in the Middle Ages, in the

Lexique de la Langue Philosophique (Paris, 1938), entry no. 84; the writing *Fī mā taqarrara . . .* by Avicenna, trans. Pines, "La Conception de la Conscience de Soi," *AHDL*, XXI, 95 ff; *Kitāb al-Najāt*, that portion in Book II, chap. 6, translated by F. Rahman in *Avicenna's Psychology*, p. 55; Abu'l-Barakāt, *Logic of Kitāb al-muʻtabar*, trans. Pines, "La Conception de la Conscience de Soi," *AHDL*, XXI, 97–98; Comtino, *Commentary on Maimonides' "Millot ha-Higgayon"* (Wolfson, *Philosophy of Spinoza*, II, 135).

46. *Commentaria in Libros Posteriorum Analyticorum Aristotelis*, i, 14 (in A. C. Crombie, *Augustine to Galileo* [London, 1952], p. 221).

47. *Analytica Posteriora*, i, tract 1, chap. 2.

48. *Opus Oxoniense*, i, d. 3, q. 4.

49. *Physics*, ii, 4, 196^b 10–13.

50. Averroes, *Tahafut al-Tahafut*, trans. S. van den Bergh, I, 316–33; A. Kamali, trans., *Al-Ghazali: Tahafut al-Falasifah* (Lahore, 1958), pp. 185–96.

fourteenth century,[51] and are particularly well stated by Nicholas of Autrecourt.

Averroes has nothing especially original to contribute to the subject of induction. He adopted Aristotle's theory of complete induction (the inductive syllogism) without modification, and added nothing to the theory of incomplete induction.[52]

There is very little evidence of a theory of induction in Christendom before there were Latin translations of the *Prior Analytics* and the *Posterior Analytics* and the *Metaphysics* (the places, as we recall, where Aristotle explicitly discusses the subject). In fact, the first work of any importance seems to be the commentary of Robert Grosseteste on the *Posterior Analytics*. In that work he states the theory which we have attributed to Avicenna, with certain enlargements. There is no doubt this commentary was one of the most widely used and quoted in later philosophical writings, and we may therefore assume that the views on induction contained therein stimulated further reflections on the subject.

Grosseteste argues as follows: (1) It is observed that ingestion of scammony is followed by the discharge of red bile. (2) This observation is repeated under circumstances in which other possible causes of the discharge of red bile have been excluded. (3) The reason now forms the universal proposition that all scammony according to its nature withdraws red bile.[53]

It is difficult to say definitely whether Grosseteste, in this passage, has clearly in mind what later will be called the Method of Agreement, the Method of Difference, or one form of the Joint Method. It is important to see that he has explicitly added some cautions about removing other possible causes of the effect to be

51. See K. Michalski, "Le Criticisme et le Scepticisme dans la Philosophie du XIVe siècle," *Bulletin International de l'Académie Polonaise des sciences et des lettres* [1926], p. 192.

52. See Léon Gauthier, *Ibn Rochd* (Paris, 1948), pp. 62, 65.

53. "Quod scammonea omnis secundum se educit coleram rubeam" (*Commentaria in Libros Posteriorum Analyticorum Aristotelis*, i, 14 [Venice, 1494, fol. 13v–14r].

investigated, and this suggests that he has in mind the Method of Difference.[54]

The clear use of something like the Method of Difference can be found in Albertus Magnus,[55] in proving that the movement of the tides depends on the movements of the moon, and he states the principle in his short work, *On the Properties of the Elements,* i, tract 2, chapters 4 to 8.

He also states the Method of Agreement, in his *Commentary on Posterior Analytics,* i, tract 1, chapter 2, and, in this connection, uses the same argument which we encountered in Avicenna, viz., we know that scammony purges bile and that wine inebriates, for the senses apprehend, for example, that inebriation frequently follows the potation of wine, and the intellect realizes that, if this were a matter of chance it would not happen frequently, and so the firm knowledge is generated that this is generally true in virtue of the nature of wine.

Thomas Aquinas has very little to say specifically on the subject of induction that is new. Lectio 20 of his commentary on *Posterior Analytics,* ii, simply expounds *Posterior Analytics,* ii, chapter 19, and adds only that some ratiocination is required in order to pass from mere experience to a principle of art or science. The reasoning in question is not elucidated but he indicates that "reason does not come to rest in the experience of particulars, but from many particulars of which one has had experience, it grasps one common thing, which is confirmed in the soul, and considers it without

54. For his use of the Principle of Parsimony, see Crombie, *Augustine to Galileo,* p. 86, and Grosseteste, *Commentaria in Libros Posteriorum Analyticorum Aristotelis,* i, 17, f. 17vb. Grosseteste did not invent this principle, of course, although he introduces it as a methodological and metaphysical principle. See *De Iride* (ed. L. Baur, "Die Philosophischen Werke des Robert Grosseteste," *Beiträge zur Geschichte der Philosophie des Mittelalters,* IX [1912], 75) and *De Lineis angulis et Figuris* (ed. L. Baur, "Die Philosophischen Werke," *BGPM,* IX, 60–61, 66).

55. See A. Mansion, "L'Induction chez Albert le Grand," *Revue Néo-Scolastique,* XIII (1906), 259.

the consideration of any of the singulars; and this common thing it takes as the principle of art and science." [56]

We can, however, gather from other statements the framework within which Aquinas must have conceived the problem of deriving universal propositions from observation. Our knowledge is derived from the stimulation of the senses, and we know the essences and powers of natural things from their manifest operations.[57] But it must also be added that our knowledge of material things and their powers is quite limited.[58] Aquinas accepts the principle of causality without question, although it is stated in a number of different forms.[59] He also accepts the principle that "In every efficient cause there must be a likeness of its effect, and, similarly in every effect the likeness of its cause must be present; for every agent produces its like." [60] This is further elucidated by the denial of genuine plurality of causes.[61] And there is, furthermore, Aquinas' view that in some sense there is absolute necessity of the causal characteristics of natural agents.[62]

We may thus assume that Aquinas' view of induction would involve a sort of inference from what occurs in particular cases to what occurs always or for the most part. There is, I think, no doubt that Aquinas sometimes wrote as if some kind of efficacy were perceptible. In any case it is evident to him that something

56. P. Conway, trans., *Saint Thomas Aquinas: Exposition of the Posterior Analytics of Aristotle* (mimeograph: Quebec, 1956), p. 430, col. 1.

57. *In Libros Posteriorum Analyticorum expositio*, i, lectio 4, and ii, lectio 7; *Summa contra Gentiles*, iii, 64.

58. *In Libros Posteriorum Analyticorum*, ii, lectio 13.

59. *Summa contra Gentiles*, ii, 15, and iii, 89 and 107; *Summa Theologiae*, Part I, q. 2, a. 3, C; *ibid.*, q. 44; a. 1, ad 1um; *ibid.*, q. 46, a. 1, ad 6um; *ibid.*, I-II, q. 5, a. 1, ad 1um.

60. *Summa contra Gentiles*, ii, 98 (trans. J. Anderson, *On the Truth of the Catholic Faith, Book II* [New York, 1956], p. 331). Cf. *Liber de Causis*, sec. 11 (O. Bardenhewer, ed., *Die pseudo-aristotelische Schrift über das reine Gute, bekannt unter den namen Liber de Causis* [Fribourg, Switzerland, 1882], p. 175).

61. *De Potentia Dei*, q. 3, a. 5; cf. *In Libros Posteriorum Analyticorum*,
62. *Summa contra Gentiles*, ii, 30, [par. 12 ff].
ii, lectios 18 and 19, and *Summa contra Gentiles*, i, 29.

undergoes movement.[63] On the other hand, it is clear that the determination of causal characteristics requires empirical investigation. This may be fairly inferred from what he tells us explicitly about the method of natural science, namely, that it involves the discovery of causes by means of their effects. The essences of natural things are known, when they can be discovered, by inferring essence from powers and powers from operation. Now as a thing whose essence is sought must be able to be recognized before we know its essence, we must use the accidents of the thing in place of its essence. If we put those two points together, it is clear that the discovery of the usual effects of things of a given kind must be discovered by noticing that things having certain accidents regularly have certain effects, or that certain effects regularly come from things identifiable through a concatenation of accidents. It is to be regretted that Aquinas did not discuss the question expressly.

Duns Scotus presents us with two interesting discussions of induction which, although they depend on Avicenna, have some nuances worth attention. In his *Questions on the Metaphysics*, i, q. 4, he holds that no experimental inference can yield a conclusion free from all doubt. For, how can a knowledge of a cause be obtained from sensible effects? Some argue as follows: If BCD are in A and it is found that D occurs without C, then AB is the cause of D. But Scotus replies, first, that if BCD are always conjoined the method cannot be applied, and second, when we have $AB\bar{C}D$ we can only say that AC is not the cause, but to say that AB *is* the cause commits the fallacy of affirming the consequent. Duns Scotus deals expressly with the inference from particular cases to a universal proposition in his *Oxford Commentary on the Sentences* (i, d. 3, q. 4). He treats exclusively of induction from singulars to universals, and does not go into the induction from species to genus. His views are something like this: We do not and cannot know all the individuals of a given species; at best

63. *Summa Theologiae*, Part I, q. 2, a. 3.

we are acquainted with only a few members of any species with which we have any acquaintance at all.

Suppose that I wish to discover, e.g., whether rhubarb cures biliousness. I can observe that, in many cases, the administration of rhubarb is followed by purgation and the relief from the symptoms of this disorder. I can then conclude that this is always the case by virtue of what Scotus describes as a "proposition reposing in his soul" to the effect that "whatever occurs in a great many instances by a cause that is not free, is the natural effect of that cause." [64] (A non-free cause is a natural cause, the only instance of a free cause being human or supra-human volition.) This proposition Scotus regards as self-evident: A natural cause by its very definition is a cause that has only one sort of effect.

We notice, as a result of experience, that natural causes of kind A are frequently followed by effects of kind B; we also notice that many cases of A followed by B differ from one another in many ways (Scotus says "For once we find such a nature [A] associated at one time with this accident and at another with that, we have discovered that despite the accidental differences, such an effect [B] invariably follows from this nature." [65]) We conclude that the effect B in question is not due to any of these accidental differences but rather to the nature A, i.e. we conclude that all A's can produce B's.

The argument has the form of Mill's Method of Agreement as applied to the discovery of the effect of a given cause. Thus suppose we are assuming that A is a natural cause and that we have

$$ABCD \ x_1$$
$$ABFG \ x_2$$
$$ABHK \ x_3$$
etc.

64. *Opus Oxoniense*, i, d. 3, q. 4 (trans. Wolter, *Duns Scotus: Philosophical Writings*, p. 109).
65. *Ibid.*

To say that A is a natural cause is to say that A has some regular effect. We discover that B is this effect because B invariably followed A amidst the varying differences C, D, F, G, H, K, etc. The argument requires, of course, certain further assumptions which Scotus does not explicitly notice. In particular, it must be assumed that we have complete knowledge of each of the observed cases of A and B.

In the technical language of the present, we can prove that B is a necessary condition of A if we assume (1) that A has *some* necessary condition, (2) that two or more cases of A differ in all respects save that B always follows or accompanies A, and (3) that we know all about the observed instances of A.

Scotus adds one qualification which explains why we must say that we are certain only that all A's *can* cause B's rather than that all A's *do* or *will* cause B's. It is that, if it is possible that the attribute by which A's have caused B's can be separated from the A's without contradiction, some A might not cause a B. In other words, if, by divine power, the normal behavior of A's could be suspended, it might happen that some A would not cause a B. We shall see that Ockham makes similar qualifications about the discovery of causal principles.

In his discussions elsewhere of causal connection, Scotus emphasizes that natural causes can be impeded so that he further qualifies the degree of certitude which we can have concerning the effects of causes. Scotus' views on induction are more expressly set forth than those of some other writers we have examined. We observe that the passage from particular cases to the universal proposition is explicitly an inference requiring a general premiss about causation. Its affinities with the doctrine of Avicenna are obvious enough: The appeal to the principle that what happens frequently is not the result of chance.

Perhaps one of the best, and certainly one of the most detailed, discussions of induction is that of William of Ockham. To understand it requires a number of preliminary remarks concerning

Ockham's general doctrines about causality. I shall begin with his views on the general principle of causality.

There is no doubt, first of all, that Ockham assumed a general principle that everything (excepting God) and every event (excepting free acts) are caused.[66] Secondly, Ockham expressly stated that the following principle is self-evident (*per se notum*): "all forms of the same kind can have effects of the same kind." [67] Ockham has several formulations of the maxim that like causes have like effects. In the Prologue to his *Questions on the Sentences* he asserts that "causes of the same kinds are effective of effects of the same kinds," [68] and this formula occurs, with slight variation, elsewhere in the *Sentences*.[69] The principle is described as being *necessary* [70] as well as *self-evident*.

The third point in these preliminaries is that Ockham allows for a plurality of causes. It is difficult to see what he means by this. The probabilities are that what he meant is consistent with the ideas of some previous writers, although the frequency with which he reiterates the point surely implies that he was in disagreement with at least some of his predecessors. As the point is of some importance it needs special discussion.

Aristotle had maintained that there is an apparent but not a real plurality of causes.[71] The logical considerations are, basically, that a property will be convertible with the genus to which it applies

66. The exception in favor of free volitions is made in *Sententiarum*, i, d. 35, q. 2, C: "Non probatur sufficienter quod omne ens est efficiens vel effectus alicuius efficientis" (*Opera Plurima* [Lyon, 1494–1496], reprinted in facsimile [London, 1962], Vol. III).

67. "Omnes formae eiusdem rationis possunt habere effectus eiusdem rationis" (*Sententiarum*, ii, q. 25, L). The reason for "can have" (*possunt habere*) rather than "have" is this: Ockham always qualifies in this way so as to allow for divine interruption of normal causal routines.

68. *Sententiarum*, i, Prologue, q. 1, subquest. 2.

69. E.g., "omnia individua eiusdem rationis sunt nata habere effectus eiusdem rationis in passo eiusdem rationis aequaliter disposito" (*ibid.*, i, Prologue, q. 2, subquest. 2, K); "causae eiusdem rationis habent effectus eiusdem rationis" (*ibid.*, q. 1, subquest. 2, JJ).

70. *Quodlibeta Septem*, iv, q. 2.

71. *Posterior Analytics*, ii, 16–18; see especially 98[b] 25–35.

uniquely. But the point is further made out in Aristotle's *Metaphysics*.[72] The ground for this view in Aristotle's thought seems to be as follows: Suppose that there are apparently two distinct kinds of cause of a given kind of effect. Since potentialities are actualized only by actualities which have the appropriate powers, the two apparently distinct causes must have some common feature, whether it is obvious or not.

Many medieval philosophers reflect this view in one form or another. Grosseteste, for example, held that of every univocal passion there is a univocal cause.[73] Aquinas is quite explicit on the point. "Even if there is no heat in the sun, there is nevertheless in it a certain power which is the principle of heat." [74] If the sun causes heat in bodies on the earth, it must have something in it like the heat it produces, even though, in this case, the cause is not ostensibly like the effect.[75]

In the case of Ockham I have found no explicit statement that plurality of causes is only apparent. It might be conjectured that he took this for granted, but this is far from proof. What is clear is that he repeatedly affirms that there can be many causes (distinct in species) of the same kind of effect.[76]

72. *Metaphysics*, Z, 8, 1033ᵇ 30 ff. The propriety of connecting this discussion with the one in *Posterior Analytics*, ii, 16–18, may not be doubted. In *Posterior Analytics*, i, 5, Aristotle points out that error in demonstration sometimes occurs because we do not have a name for the genus with which a given property is convertible; in the passage just cited from the *Metaphysics* he makes the same point. We are, therefore, justified in supposing that Aristotle holds that the genuine cause (in contrast to a "sign") which enters into a demonstration reciprocates with its effect. See also *Physics*, viii, 5, 257ᵇ 9 ff.

73. *De Calore Solis* (ed. L. Baur, "Die Philosophischen Werke," *BGPM*, IX, 79–84).

74. *In Libros Posteriorum Analyticorum*, i, lectio 6 (trans. Conway, *Exposition of the Posterior Analytics*, p. 40, col. 1); cf. *ibid.*, ii, lectios 18 and 19.

75. *Summa contra Gentiles*, i, 29. Cf. *De Potentia Dei*, q. 3, a. 5: "A diversity of causes produces a diversity of effects," and *Summa contra Gentiles*, ii, 98.

76. *Sententiarum*, i, Prologue, q. 1, subquest. 2, H; *Quodlibeta Septem*, v, q. 2; *Summa Logicae*, Part III, II, chap. 10; *Sententiarum*, i, d. 1, q. 3, N.

Even if Ockham's view of the plurality of causes is to be understood in the most radical sense, i.e., that causes different both in species and genus can cause specifically identical effects, this will occasion no difficulty. The reason is this: When Ockham speaks of "cause" this is always a singular term in the sense that one object at a time is referred to. Thus when he states that there can be many different causes (in species) of the same effect (in species), he obviously means that an effect of a given kind is caused on one occasion by one object of a given kind and that a similar effect (i.e. a numerically different but specifically identical effect) is caused on another occasion by a cause of a different kind. Now his method of induction will work whether or not there is a genuine plurality or only an apparent one.

Another preliminary observation required for understanding Ockham's doctrines of induction is his insistence that a simple knowledge of some one thing cannot, by itself, provide knowledge of another thing. This means that we cannot know the causes or effects of anything simply by knowing that it exists and what it essentially is. For suppose it is held that "if the subject were known according to its whole being then all its characteristics (*passiones*) would be known . . . and likewise, if one were to cognize a cause insofar as it is a cause (*sub ratione causae*) one would also cognize the effect." Ockham replies that "This is invalid, because to know a cause insofar as it is a cause presupposes a knowledge of the effect . . . so that the knowledge of a thing as being a cause does not *cause* a knowledge of its effect but rather is the *result* of knowing its effect." Hence he concludes that "However often one experiences in himself that he knows something perfectly and intuitively, he never knows something else by means of this knowledge unless he previously also had knowledge of that other thing." [77] In other words, in order to discover the causal characteristics of anything it is necessary to have experience of that thing together with its cause or its effect.

77. *Sententiarum,* i, Prologue, q. 3, subquest. 9, F.

The final preliminary observation is this: Ockham states clearly that the intuition or demonstration of the necessary connection of a subject and its characteristics is limited to mathematics.[78]

The main differences between the methods described by Scotus and Ockham are as follows: Scotus, as we have seen, holds that from the proposition "whatever occurs in a great many instances by a cause that is not free, is the natural effect of that cause" and the proposition that A's have been associated with B's in many cases we may infer that B is the natural effect of A.[79] This is plainly in the tradition of Avicenna. Ockham, arguing differently, holds that from the proposition that "all agents of the same infima species are effective of effects of the same kind," [80] and from *one* single case of a causal transaction involving an A and a B we can infer the universal proposition that all A's can cause B's. Several qualifications must be added if Ockham is to be correctly understood, and I shall mention them shortly. Here I am only interested in the contrast between the methods of Scotus and Ockham. The main qualification that must be made is this: we must be quite sure that all possible causes of the effect B other than A have been removed. We first begin with the absence of an A and then introduce an A. If B results we can say that *this* A caused B. Then, by way of the universal principle aforementioned, we can infer that all A's can cause B's. It is clear that this is a form of what, since Mill, is called the Method of Difference, whereas Scotus' method is a form of the Method of Agreement. Also, from their own statements it is clear that Scotus was concerned with the effect of a given cause, whereas Ockham was concerned with the cause of a given effect.

The qualifications which must be made are set out below. First of all, Ockham does not seem to assume that the observation of a single case reveals causal efficacy. Two reasons may be given for

78. *Summa Logicae*, Part III, II, chap. 4 *ad finem*, and chap. 12 *ad finem*.
79. *Opus Oxoniense*, i, d. 3, q. 4 (trans. Wolter, *Duns Scotus: Philosophical Writings*, p. 109). See above, p. 140.
80. *Sententiarum*, i, Prologue, q. 1, subquest. 2, L.

this: (1) In *Sentences*, ii, q. 5, he explicitly holds that no causal connection can be established beyond question because it is always possible that what we take to be a case of causal connection is actually a miracle. (2) In *Sentences*, i, d. 45, q. 1, D, he tells us (*a*) that "in order that something is an immediate cause it suffices that if the thing exists, the effect exists and if the thing does not exist, all other things being the same, the effect does not exist," and (*b*) that if these conditions are not fulfilled we would not be convinced that something is a cause, and, moreover, if we do reject these conditions as criteria we destroy all means of knowing that something is the immediate cause of something.[81] We may not infer from the fact that Ockham insists that causal judgments must be founded on "experiments" of the kind just described, or from the fact that activity cannot be observed that he supposed that causation is a matter of mere regular concomitance or sequence. There is not only no reason to suppose this but conclusive reason against it. The whole context of *Sentences*, i, d. 45, q. 1, shows this, not to mention the fact that Ockham elsewhere speaks of the causative power (*virtus causativa*).[82] We can summarize this point by saying that Ockham believed that observation of the kind described is necessary and, in the ideal case, sufficient to establish that one thing has caused another thing, that an exercise

81. *Ibid.,* i, d. 45, q. 1, D, and ii, q. 5, K, and q. 16, C; *Summulae in Libros Physicorum,* Part II, chap. 3. In at least one place, Ockham explicitly states that causal connection can be *inferred* from the *order* of events: *Sententiarum,* i, d. 1, q. 3, O: "quod ex tali ordine semper convenit inferre causalitatem in priori respectu posterioris, maxime si prius potest esse sine posteriori et non e converso naturaliter," cited by D. Webering, O.F.M., *Theory of Demonstration according to William Ockham* ("Franciscan Institute Publications," Philosophy Series No. 10 [St. Bonaventure, N.Y., 1953]), p. 156, n. 42.

82. *Sententiarum,* ii, qq. 14–15, YY. See also *Sententiarum,* i, Prologue, q. 3, subquest. 9, F: "Inter causam et effectum est ordo et dependentia maxime essentialis . . . ;" and *ibid.,* C: "Non minus virtualiter nec minus perfecte continet causa efficiens effectum suum . . . ." E. Hochstetter, *Studien zur Metapsysik und Erkenntnislehre Wilhelms von Ockham* (Berlin and Leipzig, 1927), p. 159: "Ockham hat . . . dieses virtuelle Enthaltensein der Wirkung in der Ursache anerkannt."

of power has occurred, but that this exercise of power is manifested *only* by the occurrence of an effect upon the presence of its cause.

The second qualification is that although one observation is *ideally* sufficient, in practice many observations are usually required. The importance of this qualification is clear. Although, ideally, we can infer that "all A's can cause B" from "this A has caused B" and "all individuals of the same species can cause effects of the same kind," it is difficult to be sure about "this A has caused B." For we are rarely in the position to know that nothing has changed in the situations save the introduction of A and the immediate occurrence of B. In the example which Ockham actually uses, the case of administering a herb of a given species to a patient suffering from a fever followed by the reduction or disappearance of the fever, we cannot be sure that the only difference was the administration of the herb. Hence, in many or most instances, many observations are required.[83]

A third qualification must be considered. A proposition of the form "All A's can cause B" or "this A can cause B" is not a first proposition taken from experience unless the very substance A is capable of producing B. "For if some quality residing in the herb is the principle of heating, then the proposition which predicates the curative power of every case of that quality is a first principle, and the statement 'every herb [of such and such a kind] is thus curative' would be a demonstrable conclusion . . . ."[84] In other words, we must distinguish between causal characteristics which belong to a substance of kind A and those which belong to qualities possessed by all substances of this kind. In the case in which causal characteristic belongs to the substance, experience establishes this fact. In the latter case we can demonstrate that, since

---

83. The main discussions of these questions in Ockham's writings are *Sententiarum*, i, Prologue, q. 1, subquest. 2; *Summa Logicae*, Part III, II, chap. 10; *Expositio super Physicam Aristotelis* (Berlin, cod. elect. 974), fol. 122.

84. *Sententiarum*, i, Prologue, q. 1, subquest. 2, O.

all A is Q and all Q is B, all A is B. This last qualification has an important application in Ockham's discussion of a more complex form of induction to which I now turn.

In order to establish a universal proposition to the effect that all members of a genus, G, have a causal characteristic, B, a maxim to the effect that all members of a genus can cause effects of the same kind (or to the effect that what holds of one number of a genus holds of all others) will not suffice.[85] Indeed, it is obvious that such maxims are not, in general, true, because some species of a given genus have causal characteristics that are lacking in other species of the same genus. Hence we must employ another maxim, namely, that whatever holds of every species of a given genus holds also of the genus. Hence, in order to establish a universal proposition about a genus it is necessary to show that it holds of at least one individual of every species of the genus. In the ideal case, then, we must proceed as follows: Suppose that S_1, S_2 and S_3 are all the species of a genus G_a. We discover that X_1 is S_1 and X_1 causes B. From this and the maxim that what holds of one member of a species, *ceteris pluribus* holds of every member of the species, we obtain "all S_1 is B." Similarly, if X_2 of S_2 is B, we obtain "all S_2 is B." And, finally, if X_3 of S_3 is B, we obtain "all S_3 is B." Then, since S_1 and S_2 and S_3 are all the species of G_a, and the maxim that what holds of all species of any genus holds also of the genus, we obtain "All G_a is B." The connection between the latter part of this process of inference and Aristotle's "syllogism by induction" [86] is obvious; this sort of induction requires *all* the cases, i.e., all species of the genus.[87]

However, there is an important exception to the rule that generalization involving a genus requires experience of some members of each of the species of the genus. Suppose that we know that all S_j is B because we know that all S_j has Q and we have shown

85. *Ibid.*, M.

86. *Prior Analytics*, ii, 23; *Topics*, i, 12, 105ᵃ 13–16, *et passim*.

87. Ockham's discussions of this point are: *Sententiarum*, i, Prologue, q. 1, subquest. 2, M, and *Summa Logicae*, Part III, II, chap. 10.

that all Q is B. In other words, suppose that all members of some species S_j have a quality Q which possesses a certain causal characteristic (that "all Q is B" has to be shown experimentally by showing that a given Q has B and then applying the maxim that whatever holds of one instance of Q holds of all, i.e., the causal maxim about a species, only in this case it is a species of quality rather than a species of substance). Suppose further that all the species of a genus G_b are known to have the quality Q. In such a case we do not need to examine all the species of G_b to discover whether all G_b is B, for this can be derived syllogistically as follows:

S_j, S_k, S_l comprise G_b so that $G_b = [S_j, S_k, S_l]$. Hence,

        all G_b have Q

        all Q is B

therefore   all G_b is B.[88]

Ockham has argued that a universal proposition of the form "All A's can cause B," can be inferred from the observation of a few cases (ideally, from one case) in which an A has caused B. Such an inference must be mediated by the principle that "if one A causes B then any other A under the same circumstances can cause B," so that the whole inference has the form:

1) This A has caused B.

2) If one member of a species S has a given effect K, then any other member of the species S can cause B under the same circumstances.

Hence, all A's can cause B. He describes this inference as a "formal consequence," i.e., as a universally valid inference, but he refuses to say that this is a *demonstration*. The reason is this: A demonstration is a syllogism whose premisses are necessary, essential, etc., and whose middle term is an "intrinsic" middle term, i.e., pertains to the specific subject-matter of the subject and predicate in question. The argument we have just formulated has an "extrinsic" middle term, because the means was "all members

88. This point is discussed in *Expositio super Physicam Aristotelis* (Berlin, cod. elect. 974), fol. 122.

of a species S, etc." and this proposition goes beyond the specific subject-matter of the particular subject and predicate. Hence, although a formally valid argument is involved in arguing from experience to a universal, it is not a scientific syllogism in the Aristotelian sense, and hence not a demonstration.

3 · Conclusions

I have attempted to give some illustrations of the theory of induction which medieval philosophers developed from the suggestions of Aristotle. In the main, the medieval accounts attempt to give some meaning to Aristotle's notion that intuitive reason grasps the universal from the suggestions of observation. Doubtless Aristotle, still under the influence of Plato to some extent but already free from the doctrine of transcendent Forms and hence from the doctrine of reminiscence, supposed that by some process which the mind undergoes the truth of a universal proposition is suddenly discerned after repeated observation. The medievals, however, attempted to penetrate further into the nature of this process. It must have become clear that a direct perception of causal relations is impossible. At the same time, they must have been loath to abandon Aristotle's view that the ultimate premisses of demonstration cannot be syllogized from any more primitive propositions. Hence they supposed that the apparently sudden and immediate passage from the individual cases to the unrestricted universal proposition involved an unconscious argument or inference. This solution would preserve the doctrine that the ultimate premisses are not inferred by a scientific syllogism, and would, at the same time, make some articulate sense out of the doctrine of intuitive reason. Intuitive reason becomes an unperceived inference. In general, the medieval philosophers seem to have elaborated on Aristotle's account of incomplete induction by assuming a reasoning process or inference where Aristotle spoke of νοῦς, or intuitive reason. As a piece of corroboration for this view it is worth noticing how many medievals deal with the subject of our knowledge of prime matter. As Friedrich Solmsen has argued, and to my satisfaction proved, Aristotle does have a doctrine of prime matter.[89] One of the crucial passages attesting to this is *De Caelo*, iv, 5, 312^a 30–33, where Aristotle says that "The kinds of matter must be as numerous as the [elementary] bodies, i.e. form, but form matters in such a way that one is common to all, particularly if they pass into one another . . . ." Another is the well-known statement in the *Physics*, i, 7, 191^a 8 (cf. *Timaeus* 52 B 2), where the matter underlying the elements is knowable only *by analogy*. The doctrine of prime matter was accepted by many of the medievals but there was obvious puzzlement about how prime matter is knowable.

We find in Al-Farabi the statement that the matters of sensible bodies are not sensibles. We are certain of their existence only by syllogism and apodictic demonstration.[90] Also Avicenna says that "The existence of matter is deduced from observation of substantial generation." [91]

Many of the Scholastics of the fourteenth century express agreement with this view, as does for example Albert of Saxony. Albert asks "whether prime matter is cognizable through itself?" His answer is that "matter is not cognizable through itself by a proper concept. This is proved as follows: matter cannot be cognized through itself because it cannot produce its species in the senses because it is not sensible." [92] Marsilius of Inghen (?) asks "whether prime matter is cognizable?" and replies that "prime matter is not cognizable without argument and inference. This is proved thus:

89. F. Solmsen, "Aristotle and Prime Matter: A Reply to King," *Journal of the History of Ideas*, Vol. XIX, No. 2 (April, 1958), pp. 243–52.

90. *Catalogue of the Sciences*, chap. IV.

91. *Kitāb al-Najāt*, in A.-M. Goichon, *La Distinction de l'essence et de l'existence d'après Ibn Sīnā* (Paris, 1937), pp. 378–79.

92. *Quaestiones in VIII Libros Physicorum* (Venice, 1504), q. 13.

That which is not essentially sensible is not cognized without argument and inference; now prime matter is sensible neither essentially nor accidentally, hence it is not cognizable without inference." In fact, "no process by which we come to a cognition of prime matter is demonstrable, because it cannot be demonstrated that everything does not exist from eternity, nor can it be demonstrated that everything is not generated as a whole *de novo*. Hence it is clear that prime matter is known by analogy to form by means of argument and inference which, while not demonstrative, is more probable than other ways of accounting for generation and corruption." [93] Finally Walter Burleigh [94] holds that we know that *natures* exist by an inference which our minds make albeit *imperceptibly*. Thus these authors resolve some of the puzzles about knowledge of prime matter by appeal to argument and inference, and one of them holds that the inference is imperceptible. This is an impressive parallel to Avicenna's treatment of induction.

Some very distinguished historians of science, Pierre Duhem [95] and Anneliese Maier,[96] have seen important remarks on induction in the commentaries of John Buridan on Aristotle's *Physics* and *Metaphysics*. In justice to these authors, I feel obligated to call the reader's attention to Buridan's remarks. But I must confess that I do not find them as valuable as the medieval discussions I have expounded above.

Buridan argues, in effect, as follows: One often accepts an induction from many individual cases. This is sufficient for holding the universal principle covering all the cases, provided that no counter-instances have been discovered. There is, indeed, no other way to establish such generalizations as, e.g., that fire is hot, that all magnets attract iron, that rhubarb is purgative of bile, etc.

93. *Quaestiones super VIII Libros Physicorum Aristotelis,* in *Opera Omnia Scoti* (Lyon, 1639), Vol. II, p. 84, col. 7.

94. *Commentaria in Libros Physicorum* (Venice, 1589), fols. 145–46.

95. In *Le Système du Monde* (Paris, 1954), pp. 715–18.

96. In *Metaphysische Hintergründe der Spätscholastischen Naturphilosophie* (Rome, 1955), pp. 385 ff.

Buridan also holds that the human intellect is compelled by its natural inclination to truth to concede a universal proposition by having had experience of numerous singular instances of the universal.[97]

This, in principle, is all that is to be found in the passages cited, and it must be confessed that, as it stands, it is not nearly as impressive as the doctrines of Ockham on the subject. Indeed, unless Buridan has elaborated his views in other writings, the suspicion is bound to occur to one that it was against such views that one of Francis Bacon's famous aphorisms was directed, viz., that induction by simple enumeration is puerile and is subject to refutation by a single counter-instance.

It is not within my purpose here to discuss the development of the theory of induction beyond the fourteenth century. Such views as were developed by the later Paduans and in the seventeenth century by Francis Bacon have already been adequately dealt with by J. H. Randall, Robert Leslie Ellis, Tadeuz Kotarbinski and others. The studies of Bacon have shown that he made important advances in expounding the rationale of eliminative induction over any of his medieval precursors. I have found nothing in the medieval authors which corresponds to the exact formulation of the methods of Agreement, of Difference, and of Concomitant Variation, which, in principle at least, are to be found in the second book of the *Novum Organum*. To this extent, Bacon's boast that he followed in no man's footsteps may be credited. Yet the medieval authors, as I have tried to show, made some important first steps in this direction, and their reflections are worth recording for this reason.

97. See Johannes Buridan, *Subtilissimae Quaestiones super VIII Physicorum Libros Aristotelis* (Paris, 1509), i, q. 15; iv, q. 7; vii, q. 4; *Quaestiones in Metaphysicorum Libros Aristotelis* (Paris, 1588), q. 2; *Expositio in Libros Physicorum* (Vat. Lat. 2162), fol. 12ʳ–13ʳ, cited by Maier, *Metaphysische Hintergründe der Spätscholastischen Naturphilosophie*, p. 387 and n. 16.

Index

Aaron, R. I., 14
Abelard, Peter, 4, 7, 37, 44
Abu'l-Barakāt al-Baghdādī, 134n, 135n
Albert of Saxony, 151
Albertus Magnus, St., 73, 74n, 84, 97, 114n, 119, 135, 137
Alexander of Aphrodisias, 6, 35n, 43n
Anaxagoras, 65
Antisthenes, 42
Aquinas. See Thomas Aquinas, St.
Aristotle, xi, 5, 7, 9, 13, 34n, 35n, 42, 43, 45n, 49, 55, 62, 63, 65n, 68, 69, 70–76, 78, 83–85, 93n, 95, 98, 99, 101, 110n, 122–27, 130–32, 134n, 136, 142, 143, 148, 150, 151
Arnauld, Antoine, 11, 12, 30n
al-Asharī, 135
Augustine, St., 35n, 87, 100
Averroes, 8, 90n, 94, 95, 134, 135n, 136
Avicenna, xii, 7, 89, 91, 92, 93, 95, 96n, 100, 101, 114n, 128, 133, 134, 135n, 136, 139, 141, 145, 151

Bacon, Francis, xii, 121, 123, 153
al-Baghdādī. See Abu'l-Barakāt al-Baghdādī
Baron, Robert, 13
Basil, St., 87
Berkeley, George, xi, 3, 4, 5, 10n, 13, 14–32, 35–37, 39, 40, 41, 42, 52, 53, 57, 60, 113, 114

Boethius, 6, 7, 30n, 37, 43, 72, 88, 89, 100
Bonitz, Hermann, 130
Boyle, Robert, 14n
Brandt, Frithiof, 28–29
Burgersdick, F., 13
Buridan, John, 152, 153
Burleigh, Walter, 152

Celsus, 134n
Church, Ralph, 36
Cicero, 134n
Clarke, Samuel, 14n
Cornford, F. M., 67

Democritus, 65, 78
Descartes, René, 12, 14n, 18, 35, 41, 112
Dionysius the Areopagite, St. See Pseudo-Dionysius
Dioscorides, Pedanius, 134n
Duhem, Pierre, 152
Duns Scotus, Johannes, 44, 45, 50, 73, 74n, 77, 100, 101, 102n, 103, 104, 112, 124, 135, 139, 140, 141, 145
Durandus de Sancto Porciano, Gulielmus, 35n

Eleatics, 64, 65
Ellis, Robert Leslie, 153
Epicureans, 81, 82, 129
Epicurus, 82, 129
Eriugena, Johannes Scotus, 89

Eustratius, 130*n*

Fakhr al-Dīn al-Rāzī, 90, 97*n*
al-Fārābī, 75, 151
Fraser, A. C., 31*n*
Frege, Gottlob, xii, 117

Galen, 130*n*, 134*n*
Gassendi, Pierre, 113
al-Ghazālī, xii, 8*n*, 90*n*, 133, 134*n*, 135
Giles of Rome, 35*n*
Gregory of Rimini, 108, 109, 111, 112
Grosseteste, Robert, 133, 135, 136, 143

Hackforth, R., 66
Henry of Ghent, 35*n*, 100, 101, 105
Herodotus, 134*n*
Hervaeus Natalis, 35*n*
Hippocratic corpus, 122
Hobbes, Thomas, 29, 37, 41, 45*n*, 113
Hobhouse, L. T., 116
Hugh of Saint Victor, 14*n*
Hume, David, xi, 3, 4, 13, 19, 20, 21, 23, 24, 29, 32–42, 49, 52, 53, 56, 57, 60, 114, 115, 116, 129

John of Salisbury, 7, 30*n*

Kant, Immanuel, 116
Kotarbinski, Tadeuz, 153
Krempel, A., ix, 72*n*, 74*n*, 94, 98

Leibniz, Gottfried Wilhelm, Baron von, 41, 77, 97*n*, 114
Leucippus, 65
Locke, John, 5, 11, 13–18, 21, 22, 23, 28, 32, 36, 41, 59, 113
Lucretius, 81

Maier, Anneliese, 152
Maimonides, 90, 93, 94
Marsilius of Inghen, 151
Martin, Gottfried, ix, 74, 85, 106
Melissus of Samos, 64, 65
Mill, John Stuart, 126, 140, 145
Mutakallimūn, 89, 90–93, 95, 96*n*, 134

Neoplatonists, 79, 82
Nicolas of Autrecourt, 45*n*, 136
Nicole, Pierre, 12, 30*n*

Pacius, 74*n*
Paduans, 153
Peirce, Charles S., xii, 117
Petrus Aureoli, 109
Petrus Hispanus, 14
Philoponus, John, 126, 130*n*
Plato, 42, 43*n*, 63, 66, 67, 72, 80, 84, 86, 122, 123, 150
Pliny, 134*n*
Plotinus, 63, 79, 80, 82, 83, 84, 85, 93, 96*n*
Porphyry, 43
Price, H. H., 57
Proclus, 9
Pseudo-Dionysius, 89

Quine, W. V., 54

Randall, J. H., 153
Reid, Thomas, 30, 39
Roscelin, 4
Rufus of Ephesus, 134*n*
Russell, Bertrand, xii, 56, 58, 117

Sceptics, 129
Scheibler, Christopher, 13
Schroeder, E., xii, 117
Sextus Empiricus, 79, 80, 129, 134*n*
Sieburth, Gunther, ix, 78
Simplicius, ix, 63, 75, 79, 80, 82, 85, 86, 91, 93, 96*n*, 100, 101, 106
Solmsen, Friedrich, 151
Spinoza, Baruch, 41, 112
Stewart, Dugald, 4
Stoics, 63, 78, 79, 80, 81, 82, 85, 91, 96*n*, 128, 129
Suarez, Francisco, 13, 19*n*, 28, 35*n*, 97*n*, 99*n*, 114*n*

Themistius, 130*n*
Theophrastus, 62, 134*n*
Thomas Aquinas, St., 7, 8, 9, 10, 11, 14*n*, 18*n*, 19, 23*n*, 30*n*, 45*n*, 48*n*, 72, 74*n*, 84, 95, 98, 99, 100, 114*n*, 119, 128, 137, 138, 139, 143

Van den Bergh, Simon, ix, 8*n*
Vignaux, Paul, 4, 7, 44

William of Ockham, xi, 4, 11, 14*n*, 29*n*, 33, 34*n*, 35, 37, 40, 44, 45, 46–53, 54*n*, 55, 56, 58, 60, 73, 102*n*, 103–9, 119, 135, 141–47, 148*n*, 149, 153